A MAN SHORT

A MAN SHORT

An Insider's Tale of
T.G.I.Friday's in the 1980s

JEFF RYAN

While the incidents in this book did happen, some of the names and personal characteristics of some of the individuals have been changed. Any resulting resemblance to persons living or dead is entirely coincidental and unintentional.

A Man Short: An Insider's Tale of T.G.I.Friday's in the 1980s
Copyright © 2009 by Jeff Ryan
All rights reserved. No part of this book may be used or reproduced in any form, electronic or mechanical, including photocopying, recording, or scanning into any information storage and retrieval system, without written permission from the author except in the case of brief quotation embodied in critical articles and reviews.

Cover design by Matthew Garza
Author photo by Melissa Mykal Batalin
Book design by Melissa Mykal Batalin

To order additional copies of this title,
contact your favorite local bookstore or visit www.tbmbooks.com

ISBN: 978-1-61584679-5

Dedicated to my Aunt Dottie,
who in a written note proclaimed:
"There is a book in you."

ACKNOWLEDGEMENTS

People enter the Hospitality Industry from many different directions. For me, it was a chance encounter with a fellow named Ken Gerew almost forty years ago. Today, we remain the best of friends.

I may not have accepted a position with T.G.I.Friday's if it were not for the unselfish prodding of Linda Miller. Words cannot express my gratitude.

My thanks to Walt Henrion, Frank Steed and Eric Scoggin for providing valuable input on the company not the least of which were the beginnings of Friday's on Greenville Avenue in Dallas, and The Potato Skin Story.

Finally, thanks to Jon Healey and John Blocker for their contributions to the humorous side of *A Man Short*.

PROLOGUE

Your fourth grade teacher may have proposed the same question to your class as she did to mine. "Students, I would like each one of you to tell the class what you would like to be when you grow up." As she prepared a section of the blackboard to receive our answers the room filled with chatter. This was a question that caught everyone by surprise. She chose our row to get things started. Charlene Nixon wanted to be a nurse, Sandra Ott a school teacher, and next it was my turn to answer. "Jeff, how about you?" she asked.

"I would like to be a tug boat operator." She paused as if to say, 'Are you sure that is what you want to say?' She made the entry on the board: Jeff Ryan, Tug Boat Operator. Moments later she saw that my hand was raised again. "Yes Jeff?"

"Mrs. Haslett, may I change my answer?"

"Well I suppose you may," she said.

"I would like to be President of the United States."

If memory serves me correctly, not one person in the class mentioned the hospitality industry. At least no one in my row anyway. When asked where I got my start in this business, I have always proudly replied, "I got my high-altitude training with Friday's back in 1981." In reality, however, that is not the whole story. I would have to return farther back to 1970, when at the age of 20, unhappy with my college commute to Northeastern University and with less than a stellar academic performance, I was in search of a change of scenery. I thought perhaps Fort Lauderdale was the place. Knowing that the best time to approach my father on matters of importance was during his morning shave, I did so. Armed with a curt blessing to ("go ahead and give it a shot") with a wholesome disclaimer of "your mother will not be happy," I left our home in South Weymouth, Massachusetts and flew south on National Airlines to sunny Florida. Here my first opportunity in the hospitality industry presented itself.

At the recommendation of Al Denly—a larger than life character—who, along with our family, was a fellow member of Wollaston Golf Club, I was to stay on Al's Ft. Lauderdale based houseboat until I could find an apartment. It was from this new base of operations in Ft. Lauderdale that I learned of an available apartment at The Square Rigger on nearby Isle of Venice, and it was from this move that my new life in the hospitality business took shape.

At The Square Rigger I had the good fortune of meeting Ken Gerew for the first time. A Rochester native, he and his wife Candy were live-in managers of the building and adjacent dock. Noticing that my possessions were pretty much limited to my golf clubs, he invited me out for a round of golf at Rolling Hills, the first of many over what has now become a lifelong friendship, and after the round we stopped at Henry's, a watering hole just around the corner. Ken informed me that he was a part-time bouncer at The Scene South, a large night club located close to the Airport on AIA. He suggested that he might be able to convince the manager to hire me as a bartender. Without a car and just under the legal age, behind the bar I went.

Up until this time my experience with nightclubs had been limited to slipping into places like Lucifer's in Kenmore Square, certainly a worthy adversary, though not quite on the scale of the Scene South. It was one of three Scene clubs in existence in

1970s, the others The Scene North on Erie Boulevard in Syracuse and The Scene West on Houston's West Alabama Road. Fresh out of college, Scene owners Jim and Dick Fraser opened their first club in Clifton, Ohio not too far from The University of Cincinnati's campus. Modeled after a highly successful disco on Peachtree in Atlanta, a lighted dance floor built of Plexiglas, a giant mirror ball hanging from above, studio quality music, and large projection screens were all incorporated into the Scene experience.

Down in Florida, the remote airport location most likely was the club's undoing. However, undaunted, the brothers Fraser were not about to give up on us. A converted warehouse at 2525 Walden Avenue in Cheektowaga (Indian translation: land of the crab apples), New York would be our next opportunity to prove ourselves. We weren't eager to leave beautiful Florida for grim upstate New York, but when you are in your early twenties climate does not matter as much. Besides, this business was about late nights and sleeping until noon. It didn't really matter where we were.

Buffalo surprised everyone. It was one of the most high-spirited party towns we would ever encounter during our 8 year run. It was not uncommon to see 1500 people walk through the door on a Monday night, and on weekends, half the crowd was from Canada. Every square inch of the 100 foot long dance floor was occupied. We learned early on that the key to this business was to keep these huge crowds entertained, especially with discounted drink promotions. An evening at Uncle Sam's was, in a nutshell, a 4 hour aerobics class with whiskey.

After management assignments in Detroit, Michigan and Cranston, Rhode Island, a newly created position of Expansion Director presented itself, officially launching my career in site selection. On September 17, 1974, with my trusted Irish Setter, Colonel, riding shotgun, we hit the road in my Sumatra Green

Volkswagen Beetle. In those days, once we secured a site, we would stay and supervise the construction. My first site was in Knoxville, Tennessee and the last in that role was in 1978, in Levittown, Long Island, New York.

As the '70s wound down, so did the disco era. I began to think of other future routes in site selection. It was in 1978 that I first made contact with Friday's, and although they had no plans to add to their staff at this point, I was asked to keep in touch.

In the interim period and after many rounds of golf that summer, I had sent for the Boston Sunday Globe in order to peruse the want-ads. Digital Equipment Corp., or D.E.C. as it was affectionately called, was looking for a Site Selection Specialist for their new retail project, The Digital Computer Store. I thought, why not give them a call. D.E.C. was the kingpin of the small computer business in those days second only to IBM in sales, and a Fortune 500 Company. A small fleet of helicopters ferried personnel to and from various offices and even to their own landing gate at Logan Airport. This new Retail Division was a swat team of veteran executives based in Merrimack, New Hampshire whose marching orders were to find prime downtown retail locations in a hurry.

My interviews went well, and we were off to the races. This time, travel was a bit different. Colonel was left at my mother's house with her beloved dachshund Schultz, and I raced off to Logan. The drill was simple. Sylvia, my assistant, handed me my travel itinerary, plane tickets, etc. on Monday at noon. A typical itinerary might include meeting with Coldwell Banker in L.A. and coming back with a deal to present the following Monday morning. There was very little in the way of negotiation; the idea was to just bring back the best site and the rest would be handled at home. I was carrying around photos of the store, but the real interest was generated when I flashed a financial statement from a Fortune 500 Company. Developers and brokers could not believe that folks from such a large company could turn around a deal so fast. (Truth is, neither could I until I witnessed it.) I would present the location to the group on Monday, Kirley—in house attorney—would finalize the deal on the phone, and Sylvia would send out a lease the same day. A construction person was at the site by Wednesday, and, bang, onto the next city.

How did this madness come to an end? D.E.C. built the stores—perhaps 20 of them—before they had the right product on the shelves. Their target was the small company of 50 employees or less: doctors, lawyers, accountants, but they had yet to develop the software applications for these folks. Perhaps the digital retail store was way ahead of its time. We did not have the time to ask when and where buying decisions were made. Were decisions made on weekends? Would the customer prefer a mall location? It all went up in smoke in less than one year.

It is time to check back with Friday's.

Blaze Bomberkoff called to say that he was flying into Cincinnati and that I could meet him at Friday's in Springdale. He was holding a Chivas in one hand as he greeted me that evening, which I would come to learn was a characteristic pose for him. We both felt that with his guidance, I could catch on relatively fast. Mike Hardinballs, Vice President of Real Estate, saw the potential of a one-two combination of Bomberkoff and Ryan covering the Northeast Corridor, from Philly on up to Boston. Friday's viewed this unexplored region much like wildcatters view The Permian Basin.

This book is about my time on the road with four unique and true to life characters in our quest to undertake the most ambitious expansion plans of any dinner house company of its time. The action will take us directly from Friday's Headquarters in Dallas to seven Northeast locations that were opened in the mid 1980s, along with a few exciting stops along the way.

ONE

The Working Map

> "To insure the company's growth, we need to have quality-paced growth of our internal concepts. I'm going to run the company without the pressures of the marketplace. I'm not going to yield to multiples or anything else. We're going to yield only to that rate in which we can absorb units. If we start having difficulty, we're going to throttle back. If we're able to absorb more, we're going to push forward, but it is going to with be an eye towards quality growth within the company."

Viken Dane, President and C.E.O.
(Remarks to the Danish Society of Kings, sometime in the 1980s)

Viken's words were both prophetic and ominous. The 1980s were looking very bright. Sales at Friday's on Newbury Street in Boston were twice our national average with hardly a sign of slowing down, and suburban stores in Woodbridge, New Jersey and Westbury, Long Island were running on jet fuel. Our Headquarters on Midway Road in Dallas was abuzz with activity. A second concept called Dalt's was stretching its legs, conceptual plans for a fast casual concept were removed from the drawer, and there was an I.P.O. in the offing.

The company, however, was about to embark on its most ambitious growth to date. Our orders were to open twenty restaurants in 1984. Was this doable? Was it insanity? Who gave the order?

> *"Forward The Light Brigade!"*
> *Was there a man dismayed?*
> *Not tho' the soldiers knew*
> *Someone had blundered:*
> *Theirs not to make reply,*
> *Theirs not to reason why,*
> *Theirs but to do and die:*
> *Into the valley of Death*
> *Rode the six hundred.*

A gorgeous spring day was about to unfold in Dallas. It was April 6, 1981 and my first day on the job as Regional Director of Real Estate for T.G.I.Friday's. "Jeff Ryan's here, we didn't think you were going to show," bellowed Mike Hardinballs as he rose from his chair to shake my hand. "Come on, Ryan, follow me. You've met Betty Baker, our trusted Administrative Assistant. That's your desk next to Blaze's. You guys will be traveling in the same direction so we thought it wise to bunk together. He's not here today, been up in Philly grinding away. Go ahead, set your briefcase down for a second; and let's meet the rest of the guys." There were plane tickets on my desk. Must be going somewhere? I wondered. "Meet Sherwin Bliss and Claus Von Blucher. We felt that we needed to hire a couple of Texans for morale purposes. They will be working the southwest where I can keep a close eye on their progress. Then we'll spring 'em loose. Bewly," he knocked, "are you in there?" He was. "Say hello to Tom Bewlinski (The Silver Fox)."

"Welcome aboard... my friends call me Bewly."

"Ryan," Hardinballs said, "we thought the best way for you to get you started would be to spend the week with this guy out in Los Angeles. You can learn from one of the best, right Bewly? You can grab your things at The Crowne Plaza on the way to D.F.W. The plane tickets are on your desk."

Bewly pulled in front of the hotel lobby. He asked as I got in, "Have you checked out the lounge, Ryan?"

"Hadn't had time, just got in last night."

"We'll stop in on Friday when we come back. Blaze and the rest of the guys will be there. You're going to see some good looking dollies."

At D.F.W. airport, Bewly launched into his pre-flight routine. It began with a stop at the airport florist where he purchased a half dozen roses. They would be going to a targeted group. Upon boarding the plane he personally saw to it that each flight attendant received a rose.

After our evening's work was finished Bewly confidently sashayed into the hotel bar—only to find American Airlines finest holding court. What a coincidence!

This was incredible. After all, it wasn't too long ago that I was driving a VW Beetle from town to town in search of disco locations with my loyal, four-legged pal, Colonel, riding shotgun. This was a step up.

Friday's had opened a unit in the relaxed waterfront community of Marina Del Rey, in 1977 and followed up with a second on Canoga Park Blvd in Woodland Hills three years later. Beginning with this trip to L.A., the company was looking for more bang for its buck out of this sprawling market and was counting on us to fill in the blanks. We had a lot of ground to cover so, the next day, Bewly thought we ought to get rolling at 10a.m., reasoning that most of the rush-hour traffic would have cleared out by then. Riding shotgun, Bewly handed over The Working Map, probably the most valuable in-house tool that we produced on the road. It was this finished product that reflected our work in the field and that was brought back to headquarters. In actuality, several maps were marked up while underway, while the clean map was back at the office ready for final drafting. Blaze was the best cartographer of the group, with meticulous handwriting, multi-colored highlights, the works.

What was on these maps? Highlights of residential neighborhoods in the form of dollar signs. For example, Beverly Hills would receive $$$+ for Upper Crust, Thousand Oaks $$$ for Upper Middle, Brea $$, and on down the line. M/F 400 would signify an apartment complex with 400 units. Marina Del Rey had over 10,000 boat slips so draw a sailboat and put the corresponding number next to it. C.B.D. in big block letters stood for Central Business District. Arrows pointed towards new growth. Major retail and office complexes were identified, as well as dinner houses, hotels, and even industrial areas. Call it an exercise in the process of elimination if you will, as, once complete, we would know where *not* to build.

It was not uncommon to drive 1000 miles or more to finish what we came to accomplish, and that was to know a market cold. We were only going to do this exercise once, so the goal was to leave no stone unturned and take nothing for granted. Backtracking was not an option. We were on a reconnaissance mission and did not want to blow it for the big invasion yet to come.

We hardly ever stopped for lunch, but the evenings were a different story. A retired Wall Street executive told me once that a lot of his information gathering took place at night, so much so that he didn't take a solid shit in twenty years. If twenty years at Friday's was a cause of that type of thing, I didn't mind too much. There was not a restaurant, bar, saloon, or information-gathering nighttime opportunity that did not attract our attention. My match collection will attest to that.

As evening approached, Bewly, all business for most of the day picked a spot where he thought in the back of his mind we could do some bonding. Cruising down Santa Monica Boulevard, Bewly asked me if I had ever been to a Turtle Race. I hadn't been to one, nor did I know what it was, so Bewly decided we would go. "There's a place called Jack's up on the left hand side. They usually stage the races outside in the parking lot. Let's go check it out," he said. Well sure enough they were setting up the course as we pulled in. A huge circle was being drawn in chalk and the starting gate was the center. It was obvious to me that the first turtle that made it outside the circle was the winner. We used to do off the wall promotions in the night club business, but this was a first.

Inside the bar, (packed with, what you would call them? "Turtle Enthusiasts?") Bewly grabbed a couple of beers. "Okay, Ryan, you are going to be approached by turtle owners who are going to claim that they own the fastest turtle in the joint. They're going to want you to buy their turtle. If you do, then you can enter it into the race." I was confused. Wasn't a turtle just a turtle? How do you handicap a turtle? You don't necessarily look at its teeth like you would a horse. They are all slow aren't they?

Bewly could tell I was confused. "I guarantee you," he said, "that there is one in here that is a ringer." Okay, I was in. "What do you get if you win?" I asked.

"A trophy," he replied.

"A trophy?"

"Yeah, you can put it on your desk," he snickered.

"That's fine," I said, my interest growing every minute of this hilarious proposition. "What about the turtle, does he fly back to Dallas with us, or does he end up in a bowl of soup?"

The race wasn't going to start for another 15 minutes. Sure enough, a young man wearing a U.C.L.A. sweater and holding a decent sized turtle approached the two of us. "Hey man, let me introduce you to Max, the fastest turtle in the place. I would know," he said, "I raised him myself ever since he was little. Follows me around the dorm, even into the shower. Don't believe in keeping him cooped up in a cage man," he went on.

I had to ask a few questions. "I'm just curious, what does Max like to eat?"

"Fruits and vegetables, whole grain cereal, but no dairy!" his proud owner replied.

"Well, he looks ready," said Bewly. "I mean look at him."

"Go ahead, hold him," said Mr. U.C.L.A. "See that, he likes you guys," he said. Bewly wisely handed Max over to me. "Ryan," he said, "go ahead and make a bid."

"Okay fine," I said. "I'll give you twenty bucks for him."

"Done deal, dude. Here he is," and he handed him over. "Max, I'm going to miss ya!" I later learned I could have gotten him for a ten-spot.

An announcement was made that it was five minutes to post, so it was off to the parking lot with Max. Bewly gave him a pep talk before we handed him over to a race official. "Come on, Max, make us proud." Max had been assigned #7 out of 10 turtles entered. They were placed in a circular corral that, when lifted, starts the race to the outer ring. That is, if the turtle didn't get stage fright!

The crowd was now three deep around the outer ring and making a lot of noise. Was this Max's first race? We forgot to ask if he had any prior experience. Had we been had?

Finally, the gates opened and the turtles were free to run. "Over here, Max!" we called, as if he is going to recognize his name. Now I've got myself wondering: will a pet turtle come when called by his name? The good news was that his head was sticking out and moving side to side. Perhaps he was looking for his [former] owner in the crowd. "Come on, Max, we are over here!" I yelled, as I started waving to my new pet. Max got all fours going and made a beeline to the outer circle. Wouldn't you know it, he won.

"Winner, #7, let's hear it for Max!" the announcer declared. There was the trophy presentation, of course, along with a photo session. "Ok Bewly," I said. "Let's go make a deal with our man from U.C.L.A. He'll want to buy him back."

"Hey man, you were right all along!" I told Mr. U.C.L.A. "Listen, we live in Dallas and won't be able to take Max home with us. Would you be interested in buying him back?" we asked.

"No, man, but thanks for asking," he said.

"Oh, okay, well how about if I just give him back to you?" I asked.

That worked. "Sure man, cool!" and we returned Max to his rightful owner. We kept the trophy.

Aside from speaking with customers, bartenders were a terrific source of information, invariably directing us to try this or that "hot spot" in town, or tell us about a new restaurant under construction. A large percentage of our job was detective work, and asking the right questions became an art form. A nightcap at the hotel bar we found especially productive, as, invariably, we would catch a lonely bartender who would speak to us uninhibitedly about any subject matter under the sun.

The most important notation made to the map, or a notation that received the most attention, was the 100% location. In other words, if you could fly a building into the market, where would you land? It did not matter what, if anything, occupied the site; we simply marked down 100%. This was our bulls-eye; this was the goal. Of course in L.A., there were several targeted markets, so more than one 100% location made its way onto the map.

If the 100% was not obtainable, we simply spread our wings

in each direction, all the while asking ourselves if this move away from the bulls-eye continued to make sense. Here is where we had to tread with caution and make sure not to, under any circumstances, allow ourselves to get out positioned or what we referred to as getting "Cut off at the Pass."

The finished maps always remained at Midway, ready at Betty's fingertips should anyone ask to see one. Viken's office put them to good use when looking for vectors on where to find that hot new restaurant. Brigid Slice, Viken's able assistant, from time to time might call down and ask us about a new restaurant that he would want to visit. If Viken asked about Ivy's in Santa Monica for example, we would say, "Oh yeah, we know where it is, Bewly and I were there last week. Let me show you the menu!"

Callers—and there were many calls into the Real Estate Department—were often pleasantly surprised that we possessed this plethora of market knowledge. Stands to reason. We had likely just driven every square inch of that market!

Our first team gathering took place at the Crowne Plaza Bar. It was time to get to know the guys. "Ryan, how was your trip with The Silver Fox? Learn anything?" Bewly, with George Peppard looks and still in his early thirties, sported a full head of pre-mature grey hair.

"Well, he sure has some style when it comes to the ladies!"

"Oh, don't tell me he came out of the box with his flower routine. He's got all the moves."

Claus steps in, "Wait until you see him tear a hundred dollar bill in half, hands it to a girl and says 'The other half is yours —if you come over to my apartment.'"

"So, Sherwin, Claus, you guys from Texas?"

"You bet, right here in Dallas. We've been with Friday's about six months. Kind of a diverse group, wouldn't you say? Hardinballs did not want to bring in a bunch of 'Real Estate Know-it-alls.' You see Friday's has its own way of doing things and I guess he feels that with the proper amount of training, we can all get the job done."

Claus continued "Shit, look at Blaze here. A Xerox transfer from Erie, PA of all places. Blaze, are you the senior member of this elite group? Shit Sherwin is... how old is Sherwin now? 36? Look across the bar, Bewly with a brunette. Guarantee you he is giving her his favorite line."

"What might that be?"

"He just asked her, 'Do you know what I like about you?' she shakes her head, and then he says 'You go with everything I wear!' Say good night to Bewly, we aren't going to see him until morning."

Sherwin jumps in "Well, boys it's been a pleasure, but this guy is headed home to his lovely wife! Ryan, great to have you on board. This group will have a lot of fun together, that I can promise." These Friday evening get-togethers would be common place from this point on.

Much like a newly formed bomber crew, the training runs continued with Blaze and Bewly alternating as pilots. We flew everywhere. Harrisburg, Des Moines, Minneapolis, St. Paul, and even into Canada. Friday's had fielded several inquiries from Canadian developers.

Meanwhile, an astute Toronto businessman had registered the Friday's trademark without any intention of building a restaurant. Smart move, ay? Efforts to reclaim the name by way of negotiations had reached a stalemate. Midway plotted a new course of action in a bold attempt to shake this guy out of the tree, a pincer movement of sorts. The plan was to send a Real Estate person to Toronto to find a high profile location where we could build a flagship store for all of Canada to see. To hell with the name, we'll call it Fred's or Bill's Place; it didn't matter. Let's see if this A-Hole can live without us now!

As a rule, the first visit to a market was always a clandestine operation. Fly under the radar until The Working Map is complete and the 100% location is identified. It was Friday's way of 'taking ownership of the market' and the only way to do this effectively was to keep distractions to a minimum by not letting anyone know we were in town until after we returned to Dallas. Uncharacteristically for us, the Toronto visit would be different. We issued an advanced warning to our colleagues in the real estate world that we were headed their way. Again for the sole purpose of shaking this guy out of the tree.

Bewly invited me to join him on the trip. "Why Canada?" I asked. "Because I saw a sign 'Drink Canada Dry,'" Bewly replied. Clever enough. The Lincoln Town Car was our car of choice, a luxury that for a few dollars more per day we felt was definitely worth the expense. This car was a living room on wheels. Passengers, especially Viken and crew, appreciated the fact that we took the initiative to chauffer them around in a roomy car.

Our game plan was to drive Toronto's perimeter first and then head for downtown. The roles were reversed this time as Bewly took the co-pilot seat and control of the working map. Working our way back into the city on lengthy Yonge Street, we started evaluating the competition with downtown Toronto off in the distance. This pub crawl from afar became quite festive as we bopped in and out of places, inching the Town Car towards our final destination, a hotel at Yonge and Bloor.

You may remember Red Buttons in the Dean Martin Celebrity Roasts when he coined the phrase "Nevva Gotta Dinna." It is safe to say that we rarely got a dinner on the road. We viewed dinner just as we did lunch: as a total waste of our time. Seldom did we sit down and fire up a nice bottle of red with a great steak. (By the way, Friday's had a terrific N.Y. Strip back then, hand cut to our specs by a company in Ft. Worth, reading from our menu: 1. Choice aged beef, hand-cut and charbroiled to perfection with Maison butter, 2. a platter served with baked potato, a large Friday's onion ring, crisp dinner salad and garlic toast. All for $10.95.)

Instead we were grazing, much like a herd of cows slowly but surely heading for the barn. At this late point in the evening, Bewly spotted a Jack in the Box and instructed me to stop. It wasn't until at a red light on Yonge Street that I had an opportunity to examine what Bewly had ordered from the menu, causing me to momentarily lose sight of what was in front of us, when suddenly, holy shit, there was a postal truck slowly rolling backwards towards us. There was nowhere to go, and my preoccupied hands were unable to find the horn in time.

Within a split second, the underside of the truck's lift gate scraped and clawed its way back over our hood. The uniformed driver dismounted from his cab and met us at the point of impact. "Sorry fellas, clutch must have slipped!" he pronounced in a distinct Canadian accent. "Almost a perfect fit, ay?"

"I'll say. What kind of rig is this?" I replied. As if small talk was going to matter!

"International Harvester Durastar 4300 Series. You've got about 25,000 pounds of truck keeping your Town Car company!" He continued, "What brings you to Canada?"

Bewly began, "We saw a sign"... at that moment, I jumped in and told the driver, "Don't mind him, he's was just trying to be funny!"

The driver's hospitality continued. "I'll pull forward, but I have to tell you, we'll be removing some more paint in the process."

"Needn't worry, it's just a rental car. In fact, before you do, just jot down your contact information just in case someone in the states needs to get a hold of you." I said. He did. "Thanks, and have a nice evening."

Both the driver and truck came away unscathed, so with his contact information in hand, Bewly thought it best to get the car to the barn before the C.M.P.'s got wind of this. We were not overly concerned about returning the car in this condition, since we figured by the time National Car Rental discovered the damage, we would be safely out of the country. The next morning, the caper was going according to plan. We parked the car in and amongst several other returns, dropped the folder in the box, and moved quickly towards the terminal, figuring once inside we could blend in with the crowd.

Our cover must have been blown as not too long inside the terminal, a green uniformed rental agent was fast approaching. Bewly and I could hear, "Oh Mr. Ryan, hold up for a second!" In the end, National charged $500.00 to my American Express Card until the matter could be resolved. Canada's Postal workers went on strike shortly after this incident, so it was going to take our folks in Risk Management some doing to get to the bottom of the matter. Incidently, we must have been bluffing as the plans to build in Toronto were placed on hold.

After L.A. and Toronto, my road work with Bewly was finished and the company was anxious to release me into the wilds of the Northeast. First there would be a coming-out party of sorts, a trip out to The International Council of Shopping Centers' May Convention in Las Vegas. Hardinballs, a confirmed bachelor with handsome features, was a classy individual with a reserved demeanor. Aware that this was our inaugural trip as a unit, he issued his only real hard and fast ground rule. Do not flaunt the company in the eyes of others. The message was clear and simple: Respect the fact that we were representing the #1 casual-themed restaurant company in America. In the same breath, I could almost hear Lee Marvin's voice inside Franco's jail cell, "If you screw up just once, then it's right back here for an immediate execution of sentence. Do I make myself clear?"

It was off to D.F.W. and Braniff Airlines. Hardinballs went solo in his Mercedes convertible, and Sherwin had the rest of us pile into his Mazda 626. Braniff, aided by deregulation, had undergone an extreme makeover. Their planes were outfitted with leather seats, flight attendants wore Halston dresses and one could fly from Dallas to Rio non-stop. We first heard the line "twelve hours from the bottle to the throttle" from Red Baron, a Braniff pilot and tavern owner in North Dallas.

This time, Bewly passed the florist shop without stopping, a sign that Hardinball's message had registered. Our impression was, however, fleeting. We later noticed that hidden inside Bewly's copy of the Dallas Morning News were several greeting cards, aptly chosen from the Missing You or Just Friends category. Each and every blushing flight attendant was issued a card. Now strapped in their jump seats, they begin the task of tearing open Bewly's envelopes as we rumbled down the runway.

We survived the convention without a mishap, and as a reward for good behavior, Hardinballs held an informal Bloody Mary Party in his suite. Shouldn't he have let sleeping dogs lie? Feeding Bewly, a devout Coors Light drinker, vodka was pretty much like starting a West Texas brush fire. There was no telling when and where it would extinguish itself.

Before long, everyone had their engines revved and were ready to go home, including Sherwin. In my short time of knowing him, we could tell he had a "go button," that deep down he was one of us. Let the antics begin. Bewly, perhaps holding on to some winnings from the tables, handed a honey-bee ($100 bill) to the first flight attendant he met with specific instructions to start spending money as soon as we were in the air. Claus, Bewly, Blaze and I took our seats in the aft section across from the galley, leaving Sherwin and Mike behind near the exit row. Blaze had identified the drawer where the liquor cache was stowed and waited until the coast was clear before raiding the neat little row of Chivas mini-bottles. He made sure to leave a few behind. Why get greedy, the flight will take a good three hours. Sherwin, a

Scotch drinker by right, peering back at us from his aisle seat could not stand being away any longer and came back to join in the festivities. Hardinballs resigned himself to let this all pass, that was until Bewly blew our cover by handing out Friday's appetizer cards for the crew to pass around.

At D.F.W., we were told that we were to meet at Midway the next morning. "Shit's gonna hit the fan, Hardinballs is pissed," I said.

Bewly diffused any notion of any serious trouble "Fella's guarantee you by morning, he will have forgetten about Braniff Airlines." Let's go get the car, I'm parched. Sherwin's car was in the parking garage one floor down on the street level.

The four of us were laiden down with garment bags and briefcases, Claus led the way onto the escalator. Bewly and Shermin followed closely behind. Somehow, after stepping onto the escalator, Sherwin's foot grabbed hold of one of Claus's bags, sending Claus face-first onto the metal, cushioned fortuitously by his garment bag which preceded his drop down. Sherwin lost his balance and ended up on top of Claus, garment bag between them and cushioning the impact. Bewly apparently wanted to join in the fun, and he too ended up falling on the pig pile. This domino effect had the three of them now stacked on top of each other, like kids on a Flexible Flyer. Claus was suffocating from the weight of two adult men on his back. We could hear Claus yelling, "Get off of me Bewly; I'm going to get sucked in!" as we approached the sidewalk. Somehow, we all made it up and off the escalator without serious damage, just some good, old-fashioned embarrassment.

Sherwin brushed himself off and asked us to stay put as he went to get the car. We could tell by his giddy actions that he was up to something! Sure enough, along came Sherwin, eschewing his normal cautious self, driving his Mazda 626 against a wall of traffic, taking a short-cut by going the wrong way. A cacophony of horn blasts started almost immediately. Accentuated by the low concrete ceiling above, the noise was deafening.

Car rental buses were all around, their drivers aghast at the site of a mad man driving recklessly on their track. Blaze, the catalyst behind this man's promotion, was prouder than a peacock watching this daredevil act unfold. "See Bewly, I told ya he'd come around," cigarette dangling from his lips and a hint of Chivas on his breath. Finally, Sherwin executed an almost perfect U-turn, stopping on a dime. "Get in; we better get the hell out of here."

Our meeting went better than expected, despite Bewly's failure to show. Hardinballs, knowing that we would each be on our own soon, was not overly concerned about a re-occurrence of any antics. In fact, he thought he was partially at fault for bringing out the Bloody Mary's at such an early hour.

It was a beautiful Friday afternoon outside 14665 Midway Road. The nearest cloud may have been in California, for all that we knew. C.E.O. Viken Dane was in a chipper mood. Invariably, when found in this euphoric state and with the weekend fast approaching, he would leave his spectacularly appointed office for a leisurely stroll throughout the building, making the first stop along the parade route in Bob Grinder's Purchasing Department, and continuing on down to Accounting and Legal, and finally up the stairs to Architecture, Construction, and Real Estate.

Once out of earshot of his longtime and loyal assistant Brigid Slice, an underground and clandestine warning system was immediately activated, "He is headed for Purchasing," she would volunteer with a muffled phone voice and soon the entire building would know of his whereabouts. Idle chatter would cease, people would return to their posts, hurriedly organize the clutter on their desks and hunker down pretending to be all business as they awaited a visit from the pontiff. It was his custom not to stop for long at any one department, allowing himself just enough time in order to maintain that important veneer of anonymity within the workplace.

It was one of these late Friday afternoon visits that he popped his head in my office and with a wry smile, opened the conversation with a comment characteristic of his way of running things, "Ryan, every time I look at you, I feel like I am a man short!" Viken could never resist a chance to bust his subordinates, myself included, but we knew it was all in good fun.

TWO

Phone Etiquette

For a first time visitor, a walk into the foyer of Friday's corporate office on Midway was much like the experience of walking in the door of one of our restaurants. One would hear "Welcome to Friday's" as you made your way up the three risers to the reception desk. The decor package was all there, hardwood floors, authentic tin ceilings, and artifacts adorning the walls. The Test Kitchen and Bar were off to the right, however concealed from view. The pleasant atmosphere would put anybody right at ease while eagerly awaiting the arrival of a host.

The reception experience was intended to be warm and inviting, both physically with the reception area and mentally with the friendly hospitality of the receptionist to visitors and callers alike. The "first impression" was going to set the tone, and a well-organized front of the house was key. There were hundreds of incoming calls each morning and afternoon, and every one was fielded with the utmost aplomb. "Good morning, thank you for calling Friday's, how may I direct your call?" Reception was a visitor or caller's first point of entry into the Friday's experience. Setting the right tone was essential.

In the Real Estate Department, our practice of handling every call was a direct result of our No-Interest Letter, which began, 'Thank you for your interest in Friday's, however due to market conditions, we are unable to consider your submittal at this time...' We did not want to impersonalize the experience of writing to us, so every site submittal from the largest and most comprehensive package to a single handwritten letter was given our undivided attention. Importantly, each and every No-Interest Letter was cordially signed by the director responsible for that particular region, and more often than not, we would find ourselves scribbling a note in the column to the effect of 'Good luck with your project' or 'Kindly check back with us in 6 months.' Treating each potential business partner with patience and individual attention was our goal; this was the service business after all.

Without exception, we always handled our own phone messages. We did not ask Betty to return calls for us. We made the calls ourselves. Why wouldn't you? How would you like to own a company and find out that your people are not returning phone calls? On the flip side, how impressed would you be if you were contacted directly by the person to whom you had placed a call?

My suggestion to Betty was to instruct people to call on Monday mornings between 9 and 11a.m. By doing so, we avoided a backlog of phone messages that would accumulate during the week. Every caller would receive the proper air time. This designated "calling hour" worked brilliantly. Over time, we all became proficient at intelligence gathering, extracting valuable market information from a caller that otherwise may have passed us by. With Blaze's desk next to mine, our office took on a newsroom atmosphere. It was like watching Woodward and Bernstein work the phones in All the Presidents Men.

A typical call might go: "Good morning, Mr. Valenti, where are you calling from? Long Beach? Out on the island? Know it well, rented a house there in 1978. No, I wasn't with Friday's at the time. The company I was with built a Discotheque on Hempstead Turnpike in Levittown. Yes, Uncle Sam's, you must have been a customer. No, I stayed on as project manager during construction. Quite an experience working in a Union environment, but it came out great. Remember that was a vacant W.T. Grant's store? Yes it was big, 15,000 square feet and we needed every inch of that. Tell me is The Salty Dog still there on the beach? Spent a lot of time there during The Lindsay Storm of 78. Snow drifts like you can't believe!" Smalltalk done, now onto business. "Yes, the Friday's in Westbury does extremely well for us. No, we actually bought that 5 acre property next to the Raceway. You are building a project in Westchester County? In Scarsdale?" Now shielding the receiver end in the palm of my left hand, a snap of the fingers sends a signal in Blaze's direction. "How about Scarsdale?" Blaze puts his phone down for a second. "Yes, great market, it's tighter than a drum but jot down his number and I will call him back this morning." I return to the call. "Let me have your phone number, Mr. Valenti, and the gentleman handling Westchester County will call you back this morning. His name is Blaze Bomberkoff. Yes, he'll definitely call you back for sure! Thanks for thinking of us."

Our success in Boston's Back Bay spawned numerous real estate related calls into our Dallas office from throughout the New England Region. There was one particular call that came into my office with an unusual request. A graduate student at Boston University called to say that she was going to write a paper on how a particular retailer determines where to locate a store, and that after consistently seeing the Back Bay location packed whenever she walked by, she chose to write about Friday's. She wondered if I would be able to provide her with an outline of what we look for in the marketplace. Suggesting that a lengthy call was in order, I called her back on our dime. She, in turn, took copious notes and thanked me for my time. A couple of months later, she called back to inform us she had aced the paper. In most instances, the person that you have befriended from afar will never meet you face to face, but we knew that he or she could be converted to a lifelong customer of the restaurant just by the way they were treated on the phone.

There was a telephone episode at Midway involving Viken, which took on an interesting twist. On a return trip from New York, I stopped by the office around 5p.m. It was customary to walk by Viken's office, and if he wasn't with someone I would say hello. This day, Brigid kind of rolled her eyes as if to say "probably not a good time to go in there." He gestured for me to come in anyway and, planting myself in a chair, I could hear that he had dialed a number on his speakerphone. As was customary, his desk was void of clutter. I remember noticing only a Friday's Store List.

I guessed right. He was calling a Friday's on the East Coast. It is a store policy that the people working the front door answer the phone within three rings or less, no exceptions, end of story. It would then have been six o'clock on the East Coast, customers undoubtedly filing in, door personnel on duty. This was a game to see who was on their toes. I wondered who he was calling. Willow Grove? The Falls in Miami? Viken was not volunteering any information, just listening intently, swiveling in his chair as if he was manning a 20 millimeter anti-aircraft gun. Brigid and I could hear ring number one, ring number two...

Silently I began saying to myself, "Come on, pick it up," but then, ring number three. Steam had begun to build up in the Viken Boiler Room, so I made my departure known and high-tailed it to safer environs. I got out just in time. Viken's phone fury continued as I heard him enlist the help of Brigid. "Call North Olmstead!" he yelled as I pushed through the doors outside. Viken would only have to walk next door to the office of his trusted Liaison Officer Buddy Busch to send a clear message to the field.

THREE

In Store Training

The best selling point we had, more so than any sales tool you could carry in your briefcase, more so than any glossy photos, menus, testimonials, financial statements, or appetizer coupons (Bewly's second favorite thing to give to the flight attendants), was the actual restaurant itself, and whenever possible, we would conduct a tour. The Management staff didn't mind too much as the sight of us there with our guests was a sure sign that the company was growing. The tours began as far back as the trench drain in the service court and ended at the front door. The only part of the restaurant that we never visited was the roof, but if we had, one would have seen the careful planning that went into the placement of the H.V.A.C. units.

In order for us to learn more about the actual day to day operation, arrangements were made for each of the four Regional Directors of Real Estate to stagger their schedules and spend a working week in an actual restaurant. We also thought that this show of detente would strengthen relations between development and operations.

For my working week, it was off to Friday's on Greenville Ave. in Dallas, site of the game changer back in 1972. This was the first Friday's built as a free-standing restaurant, which ended up becoming the norm around the country. The Greenville Ave. location was also the first to incorporate the four-sided bar, another great first for Friday's. Arriving, I introduced myself to the staff and proceeded to shadow the Manager on Duty's (M.O.D.) every movement. The M.O.D.'s first order of business was to check the log for any entries from the previous evening, including the smallest of details like "replace light bulb over bar sink" or "regrout kitchen tile near dishwasher." The Log was a red book, and every store had one. No detail was too small to make an entry and every entry warranted immediate action.

Monday morning was provisioning time for the restaurant. The "back of the house" was run almost autonomously by the Kitchen Manager (K.M.). All deliveries had to take place in the morning, without exception, and they had to be punctual. Take, for example, a produce delivery. Ten vertically stacked boxes all containing heads of lettuce arrive at the back door. The driver impatiently waits for the K.M. to scribble his John Hancock on the invoice. The K.M., not to be outfoxed, wisely coaxes the bottom box from the rest and examines the contents." We ordered green lettuce, not white," he says. "Send this one back or bring it over to The Railhead; just get it out of my sight." The other nine boxes would be inspected in the same manner.

Each day, we were learning more about the nuances of the operation, like the fact that a bar-back must work an entire year before he or she can qualify as a bartender, or, most interestingly, the stripes on the tablecloths must all point towards the front door. The direction of the stripes, the Log Book with its little notes – such things may seem trivial. However, if minor flaws slip through the cracks, then cracks become crevices and crevices become fissures.

The Log Book discipline came out of a self-examination of sorts in the mid-1970s. Leading up to 1975, the sales histories began to show that an alarming downward trend was taking form. In Viken's words, "The consumer was telling us they did not like what we were doing anymore," prompting Viken and crew to get out and see what was going on in the marketplace. They toured the country looking at restaurants, as he put it, "in all phases of success; on their way up, peaking, and on their way down, to find the common threads of success in our industry."

The passionate Viken concluded that the action that needed to be taken was right in front of our eyes: we needed to do a better job of taking care of our business rather than worry about everyone else. Changes were implemented in response. This unbridled focus on the quality of food preparation, housekeeping, repair and maintenance, and training paid off. Soon, sales bounced back. Out of this came the established philosophies, standards, and direction by which Friday's would go forward in the 1980s. In WWI, Allied Generals conducted operations from the comforts of a chateau far from the frontlines. They had no firsthand knowledge of events transpiring at the front, resulting in huge losses in men and material. Viken's decision to visit the frontlines may have saved the company.

Rocky Aoki, founder of Benihana, a chain of Japanese steakhouses, came out to Long Island to meet me one mid-afternoon at our store in Westbury. From there we were to travel to an underperforming restaurant in Manhasset that he thought could be converted to a Friday's. Rocky at the time was in Manhattan promoting his new line of frozen food products that were soon to be distributed to grocery stores. His arrival did not go unnoticed as he stepped out of a Mercedes Benz stretch limousine. Clearly, he was a fiercely competitive person both in business and pleasure. His main hobby was racing offshore power boats, a hobby not for the faint of heart.

Rocky became incensed that day seeing our restaurant full of customers this late in the afternoon, and it would not end there. Benihanas were closed during the mid-afternoon hour, and that was the case when we arrived in Manhasset. Rocky knocked on the front door. The G.M., looking straight at him through the glass door, thinking that this man was a customer, told him to come back at five o'clock. A yelling match between a C.E.O. and a G.M. ensued. We were just short of driving the limo through the front door when cooler heads prevailed. It wasn't until Rocky retrieved a business card from his brief case and pressed it up against the glass that we were allowed to gain entrance. Had Rocky become one of those Chateau Generals? We often read quotes from C.E.O.s, whose companies are in trouble."I am going to focus our attention on quality by getting back out in our restaurants." Mr. C.E.O., we can tell you from experience that by this point, you have waited too long to react. Why weren't you out there in the first place? At Friday's, we excelled in this; our attention to the ins and outs of daily restaurant life was one of the things that truly set us apart, a lesson driven home to me during my working week.

My last assignment was a Friday evening shift assisting the regular compliment of door staff. In anticipation of being O.T.L.E'd (option to leave early), my friends were invited to stop in around 9 o'clock. I was, after all, about to graduate. There is a certain sense of empowerment working the door as customers gather, tables back up, and The List grows. Servers do not want you overloading their sections as this is tantamount to bad service, which in turn compromises their ability to be tipped properly. On a smooth-running shift, you may notice a server walking by your post saying, "Come on Jeff, bring me some action to the deuce in the corner." On that night, my guests had set up shop by the bar so around 9p.m., I took a brief respite from my duties and joined them for a beer. Little did I know…

On Monday morning, the office, usually abuzz, was noticeably quiet, Betty was minding her own business, and Blaze was not his jovial self. Sherwin came into my office and said things weren't good, that I was to go down to Buddy Busch's office, and that he wanted to speak with me. When I got there, Buddy was not alone. The M.O.D. from my Friday evening shift was sitting in his office. Apparently the shift beer I had while still on duty was a clear violation of company policy and grounds for dismissal. Death by Bunga, the end. Buddy, a no-nonsense Mississippian who ironically began his career with Friday's by working the door in Memphis, had no other choice but to back his manager.

In a court of law the judge asks the defendant if there is anything he would like to say before sentencing is passed. My opportunity came with Buddy allowing me to collect my thoughts as if to say, "Jeff, think of something that may get us out of this mess." And I did. I simply said, "Buddy, I had no idea that this was a violation of company policy. Otherwise, I would not have had a beer." Buddy, sensing an opening, pounced on the opportunity to cross examine and said, "Didn't you read the employee handbook?" He reached in his desk for a copy.

The size of a USGA Rule book, Friday's Employee Handbook was 51 pages long. The last page had two signature lines below the following boldface statement: "I have received a copy of the Friday's, Inc. Employee Handbook and have read and fully understand all of the contents of the employee handbook." An employee and manager were to sign. Back on page 24: "Friday's cannot overlook an employee's violation of the rules. The following are critical rules, violation of which will result in immediate dismissal." Sure enough, there at Rule 4: "USE, POSSESSION OR BEING UNDER THE INFLUENCE OF ALCOHOL WHILE ON DUTY."

My answer was no, I hadn't read the handbook. The sentence was immediately appealed and I was told to return to my office (holding cell) and await a decision. You could have seen the movie 12 Angry Men in its entirety before my fate was determined, and perhaps the atmosphere inside Viken's office was similar to a jury room.

Buddy delivered the verdict at 10 a.m., and it read: "Ryan, you are back in, however, here is what will be required of you. At 5p.m. today, you are to attend the shift meeting and apologize to the staff. You are also to spend another week with the manager." Viken later that afternoon swung by, looked in and said, "Glad to see you could make it."

What was the management style like at Friday's in the tumultuous 1980s? First of all, the use of the terms culture, mission statement and management style are grossly overblown. 'Gee, I am thinking about going to work for you guys, what is the culture like?' Culture? What do you mean? Are we cultivating soil? What exactly is it that you want to know? 'What is your Mission Statement?' Oh, good question, let me look, I keep a copy taped to the inside of my baseball cap. Not. I have seen mission statements as long as a page and as short as two words. Ned Grace, founder and C.E.O. of Bugaboo Creek Steakhouse, Inc., soon realized that his restaurant managers were not going to effectively communicate a long drawn out epistle to their employees. Makes sense, since they themselves could not commit it to memory, just like a long, drawn out joke that has been passed around: no two people are going to tell it the same way. Ned's effective solution? Zero Defects! The most irksome thing about such terms as culture and mission statement is that they never succeed at describing what a place is all about. They fail at their core purpose.

A longtime warrior of the system, William Wallace recently gave me his version of Friday's management style. "A very hands on collaborative style of management. We were overly aggressive in our approach, as we were one of the top dogs in casual dining. *The* top dog, therefore, our ability to confront." This summed it up beautifully. To expound further, Friday's eliminated the grey areas, took away the middle ground, narrowed the playing field. There were no D.M.Z.'s, as having them in place meant that mediocrity became an option. We never heard: 'Last week's sales were okay' or 'Well, our progress has been good enough.' No, we strove for continued growth, improvement, and innovation.

I can recall a perfect demonstration of this core principle. One mid-afternoon Viken backed his Rolls Royce Corniche out of its berth at Midway and headed off to points unknown. Unless Brigid had a honing device attached to the undercarriage, there would not be an early warning. We had been around long enough to know that he wasn't going to get his nails done. Viken had slipped into Friday's at Sakowitz Village, just a scant three miles from Midway and had made it to a bar stool undetected. The father of Tom Snyder, of late night talk show fame, once told his son: "A guy that drinks at a bar in the afternoon is a bum; a guy that drinks at the country club in the afternoon is a sportsman." I guess the third possibility is that a guy going to a bar in the afternoon is there on business; Viken wasn't there to drink, nor did he belong to a country club. He began chatting it up with a bartender, who was unaware of his mystery guest's identity, other than noting that he was a nattily dressed guy probably with a lot of dough as evidenced by the Presidential Rolex on his left wrist. There were a lot of fake Rolexes floating around Dallas in those days, worn by what were called Hundred Dollar Millionaires. This was not one of them. Viken, no doubt sipping on a glass of his favorite white wine, Sonoma Coutrer Russian River Ranches, was ready to pose the question of the day, the answer to which would reverberate all the way back to Buddy's office.

'So how do you like working here?'

'Ah, its okay, it gets me by.' Enough said.

If Viken didn't know how long it took for the Corniche to go from 0-60, all he needed to do was watch the second hand on the Rolex as he powered his way back down Belt Line Road.

This was not the first time Buddy had heard what comes next. "Get back over there and shut it down, we do not deserve to be open!" Buddy would send everyone packing and reopen when the second shift arrived. Our bartender friend would more than likely resurface at a Bennigan's somewhere.

What kind of response was Viken looking for then? General Patton intimated that the important thing in any one organization is the creation of a soul which is based on pride. Viken was not so much looking for a hero worshipper, as he was for a hint of pride. A scintilla of devotion to a higher standard that would indicate to him that his message, the Friday's idea, was getting through. When a company has a great product and financial backing, then the next most crucial component is people. Good people take pride in their work, and good people keep a restaurant at the top.

Here is how we were different. Friday's was not looking for bodies, we were looking for thoroughbreds, people who could go the distance. We wanted to improve constantly, so we recognized that we needed people on our team who would buy into the program and run with it. This wasn't the Keeneland Sales where we were looking for that one Triple Crown winner; we were looking for a widespread field of talent. Each Friday's required three managers. Multiply twenty store openings (for that year) by three managers: sixty people. If a horse does not run a good enough race, it is euthanized and whisked away to the Glue Factory. Similarly, if our people didn't meet Friday's standards, which came straight out of Viken's mind, then they were gone.

On the flipside, we rewarded good work with an opportunity for advancement. The most deserving G.M.s were promoted to Regional Managers, inevitably leaving yet another void to fill in the chain. (It wasn't until years later that restaurant companies addressed the need for a retention program to keep valuable G.M.s in the store by offering a substantial increase in salary.)

A MAN SHORT

Houston's may have been the pioneer in this regard.

A major bone of contention was that most every Human Resource person that joined the company in those days was too interested in the numbers game. Because of this, Viken held HR people in disdain. Flash Peddler was no exception. Brought over from the retail sector, what was he doing there in the first place? A guy like him could clog up a pipeline faster that the zebra mussel. Flash sealed his own fate early on, the beginnings of which a few of us were there to witness.

It was Flash's maiden voyage on Triple Six Whiskey Whiskey (N666WW), the call letters for the Citation 2, a six passenger corporate jet that was hangared at Aviall, an F.B.O. at Love Field in Dallas. If Ricardo Montalban were the spokesperson for Cessna, he may have described it as a beautiful combination of tan and burgundy colors throughout, Corinthian leather seats, an elegant aircraft. Triple Six shared a hangar with Frito Lay's hardware, a Canadair 601 that quite frankly dwarfed the Citation 2. To put it in perspective, you could stand up and take a piss in the 601—not so in Triple Six.

Viken, Buddy, Blaze, Flash and I were among the passengers heading eastbound one morning. Wheels were up at 7a.m., and we had been advised by Brigid not to be late. American Airlines does not wait, and neither would our two very capable pilots, Jack Wing Sr. and Jack Jr. With all present and accounted for, we were ready to board when Flash, in looking at the Canadair for the first time, said to Viken, "When we arrive we'll get one of those." 'Shut up, Flash and get the f___ing plane' we were all saying to ourselves. Viken did not respond, other than to wonder where the hell do we they find these people.

As time went on, it became clear that Flash wasn't performing up to par. He didn't click with the group and he didn't offer any reason for the company to keep him around. Viken had a low tolerance level for anything that detracted from Friday's moving forward and going strong.

A few weeks had passed when Claus reported at one of our Friday evening get-togethers that he thought Flash was in for a beheading. Claus had hitched a ride back form L.A. and, from his position in the jump seat, he had witnessed the thrashing of Flash. No one was safe from Viken's scorn. Thinking that he might be up next, Claus buried his head in the L.A. Times as the vitriol continued to spew. Claus thought Flash would have been better off if he was handed a parachute and jumped out over the Grand Canyon.

Viken's message was very clear. Friday's wouldn't tolerate mediocre performance. Flash just didn't have it in him to go the distance. It wasn't long before he was put out to pasture.

FOUR

Cloudcroft

As is typical of any rapidly growing company, personnel changes are commonplace; it goes with the territory. Ledger Cockbill, a talented financial analyst for Buddy Busch, was elevated to the C.F.O. position, and Clavin Dunlap, an executive with a fast food company, was brought in to oversee Development. Around that time, Mike Hardinballs decided to move on, creating a vacancy at the top of our department. The architect of our Real Estate team since the beginning, Hardinballs would be sorely missed. But, better things beckoned; a beauty queen from Costa Rica, whom he met while on vacation there, had stolen his heart, leaving us without our leader.

It was quickly decided within our group that we did not want an outsider infiltrating our ranks, so the five of us hastily arranged a group meeting at our favorite off campus bar called Greenstreet's at the foot of Restaurant Row over on Composite. Hunkered down at a corner table with drinks flowing, the initial banter—as expected with any meeting, was leading us nowhere.

Breaking through the noise of our failed attempt at productivity, Blaze, a veteran of the Xerox Wars and a battle tested closer, took charge. Truth be told, he was the one with the experience and personality to lead us at that time as he proved. He snuffed out his cigarette in an ashtray and stood up, tapping the heavy bottom of his half empty rocks glass on the table as if to gavel our attention. Called to order, we listened as Blaze's husky smoker's voice delivered the brutal facts. "Sherwin," he said, "you don't have what it takes to remain in the field; you would continue to be a load. Claus, you're a wild card; however, the company has been wishy-washy about the California market in general, so see if you can come up with a couple of deals, will ya? Fuck, we might need you someday." Blaze sighed and continued, "Listen guys, Friday's has its sights on the spoils in The Northeast. It's the best restaurant market in the country, and Ryan and I are going to deliver. Now, we all know that cold weather markets limit our construction start dates. This is where Bewly comes in. He will deliver the warm weather sites out of Florida, and maybe if we catch a break, one or two as far north as Washington, D.C."

While Blaze was speaking, I stole a glance at Sherwin, shoulders slumped, deflated by Blaze's no-holds-barred assessment, sulking in his chair like a sixth grader who did not get the part he wanted in the school play. Blaze, now spitting fire, just then directed his peroration back to Sherwin. "Go in there on Monday, and ask Viken for the Real Estate Director's position." At this, Sherwin sprang to life, as Blaze laid out the terms and conditions by which Sherwin, if successful, could operate as the Department Head. "Sherwin," he continued, "you can look after Claus as you see fit and, if need be, the three of us will come to his rescue. However, under no circumstances are you to create any roadblocks for us. Do not overanalyze, do not scrutinize our travel itineraries or expense reports, as we are aware of our individual budgets. If you do as we say, we will make you look like a star!" We could see Sherwin placating Blaze by nodding in agreement, all the while thinking, "My wife is going to be so proud of me. Here I am, Sherwin Bliss, an executive for the number one restaurant company in America." Wouldn't you know it, on Monday the charade worked, and Sherwin was promoted to V.P. of Real Estate.

A MAN SHORT

Back in those days, the four Regional Directors shared two offices: Blaze and I in one, Bewly and Claus in another. Blaze was a chimney smoker, but unless we were traveling together, Monday mornings were the only part of the week that we found each other at the office together.

The Director, now Sherwin, had his own office across the hall. Looking after us all was our "Den Mother," Betty, a conservative Midwestern gal who reveled in the fact that she was babysitting for five thirty-something juveniles. It was Betty, for example, who broke the news to Sherwin that Bewly had inadvertently boarded a flight to the wrong coast, but that, not to worry, he would take the red-eye to Washington, D.C. that evening and meet the developer in the morning. Follies such as these were for the most part kept a secret, thanks to loyal Betty.

It could not have been two weeks after Sherwin's promotion that, upon arriving at the office on a Monday morning, we discovered he—at least, we assumed it was he—had redecorated his office. The distinct smell of a fresh coat of paint lured the four us to his open doorway, only to gaze in bewilderment at what we were about to see. All the guys on tiny Executive Row had nicely furnished offices, but none treated his office as if it were the Sistine Chapel. We quickly got the scoop from Betty. Sherwin's wife, an interior decorator, had come in over the weekend and applied what we were to learn was a "mauve" color to the walls—with chair coverings to match!

By now, the Real Estate team was in place as follows: Sherwin Bliss, Blaze Bomberkoff, Claus Von Blucher, Tom Bewlinsky, and me, with Betty keeping us in line. Sherwin and Clavin thought it would be a good idea to go off campus for a Strategy Session and review our individual performances. To our way of thinking this was Clavin's way to show us he was one of the guys. We were, after all, wondering how he was going to fit in coming over from the junk food side of the business and all.

Blaze, not one to pull any punches, thought it was like "putting earrings on a Buffalo."

It was up to Sherwin to determine where we would hold our Strategy Session. He could not afford to let Clavin be a witness to this circus act this early in the game. You had to give Sherwin some travel credits on this one because he did find one of the most remote spots imaginable, a hotel called The Lodge in Cloudcroft, New Mexico. A 61-room, turn of the century Victorian hideaway perched 9,000 feet up in the Sacramento Mountains; an hour's drive from Triple Six's F.B.O. in Alamogordo.

Sherwin thought it safe enough to invite Betty. She was privy to most of our exploits on the road, understandable given the tight quarters at the office, as she could not help but overhear our boisterous overtures. Now she was about to see things in a different light: live and in color.

During our off campus Strategy Session, The Lodge was home for three days. The focus of our meetings was to plot the course for the aggressive store opening plan that lay ahead. Sherwin and Clavin were to rely heavily on our ability to keep the pipeline full of site and market alternatives. Clavin was the manager of the pipeline, plain and simple. Like Sherwin, he did not have the instincts that a true site selection person would possess, but he didn't profess to either, so it was okay by us.

The only outside activity was a couple of rounds of golf at the nine hole course next door. Perhaps one of the highest elevations of any golf course in North America, the first hole had a 150-foot drop from tee to green. Of course, our other extracurricular activity was the usual nightly visit to the bar, this time the hotel bar since we were so secluded.

Two group dinners were scheduled, both at 8p.m. The first, a moderately festive affair, went off without incident. Sherwin was exuberant with only one more to go. Would this behavioral pattern hold? The following day, half hour reviews were scheduled beginning with Claus at 5p.m., Bewly next, me at 6, and on to Blaze and Betty. They were conducted in The Tower, a small seating area atop the hotel, which at the turn of the century served as an observation platform.

Claus was to lead the charge to the lounge bar; the rest of us would meet him there. Not terribly shy, he would more than likely carry on with the locals until we arrived. Well, it could have been a scene from any western movie, as Claus was sitting at a roundtable with Sheriff Hawkins. Holstering a Dirty Harry sized weapon, a 10 gallon hat resting atop the table, I could tell the two had been locked in conversation for some time. In Cloudcroft, a tiny mountain hamlet, the town's only sheriff was at ease with his newfound drinking buddy, our very own Claus. Our man could just as easily hold court with royalty at The Mansion on Turtle Creek or as in this case with The Sheriff of Cloudcroft. "Ryan, say hello to Sheriff Hawkins, pull up a chair." After removing my hand from the sheriff's vice grip, Claus continued with his interrogation. "So Sheriff, what do you do here in Cloudcroft—I mean when you are not out sheriffing?"

"We hunt and fuck," he replied.

"What do you hunt?" Claus asked.

"Something to fuck." You can imagine the laughter that ensued from there. This guy was something else.

Much to the delight of the one cocktail waitress on duty, the table grew with the arrival of Bewly, and then Blaze. Perhaps the thin air was a contributing factor to our silliness, or perhaps, still more likely, it was the home confinement feeling of The Lodge. Claus was the type to belt out his favorite tune at any ordinary moment. That night it was an acappella rendition of Moonlight Becomes You, the song that Bing Crosby sang in the movie The Road to Morocco. We never asked Claus why or when he committed the lyrics to memory. All we knew was that he loved to perform in an intimate setting and here he had just that. Drawing the song out of Claus was a relatively easy task. In this case, Bewly even asked the sheriff if was okay for Claus to sing his favorite song; now with full permission from the law, he dove right in:

> *Moonlight Becomes You it goes with your hair*
> *you certainly know the right things to wear*
> *moonlight becomes you, I'm thrilled at the sight*
> *and I could get so romantic tonight*

Even Sheriff Hawkins started lip syncing lyrics—lyrics that Bewly was feeding him in advance. Claus, now gaining confidence, continued on,

> *You're all dressed up to go dreaming,*
> *Now don't tell me I'm wrong, and what's*
> *a night to go dreaming*
> *mind if I tag along*

There is no doubt that his cavernous voice had carried up the flight of stairs leading to The Tower and Betty's review. Sherwin must have been mortified. Yet after a thunderous applause, there was only a brief respite from our bacchanalian affair. Sheriff Hawkins ordered a bottle of Yukon Jack for the table and took center stage himself. It would have been impolite for us not to partake in this welcoming gesture of 100-proof Canadien Liqueur. Soon, the waitress Otle'd herself and joined in, plopping herself down on Claus's lap. In passing the bottle after a generous tug, the sheriff read from memory the inscription on the reverse side of the label: "Yukon Jack is a taste born of hoary nights when lonely men struggled to keep their fires lit and cabins warm."

On this hoary night, the combination of Dewars and Yukon Jack was taking its toll. This was a time when you wished you had two separate tanks to fill, much like a 1985 X J6. Claus and his nubile lapmate, impervious to their surroundings, had moved on to the mauling phase of their relationship, all while remaining in the chair. The Sheriff had decided to lay his head on the table in such a manner that it seemed someone had snapped his neck in order for it to lay so perfectly on its side. Now fast asleep, one could see a bit of a drool seeping out of a crevice of his partially closed mouth.

Blaze, however, had the burners going in rapid-fire succession, a sure sign that his Chivas was going down smoothly. Blaze did not hesitate to instruct the bartender not to change the ice, but simply to build a new drink on top of the old. This may have been a first for our man behind the bar, but he caught on quite nicely. Finally, on time for the group dinner but late to the party enter Clavin, Sherwin, and Betty. Imagine the visual. Needless to say there were empty settings at the dinner table that evening.

The Lodge must have reminded Bewly of the chateau in The Dirty Dozen where the Germans were holed up. Bewly, assuming the role of Telly Savalas's A.J. Maggott, was stalking Betty, the German officer's girlfriend. In the wee hours of the morning, we could hear him out in the hallway, the squeaky floors of the 100-year-old Inn not letting anyone go undetected, then the faint knock on her door. Betty, very married, had to be flattered that she was attracting so much attention, but she wasn't about to succumb to A.J.'s advances. Nonetheless, he tried. "Who is it?" Betty answered. "It's me, Bewly, open the door." No luck, but rest assured, had Bewly succeeded, they could have tossed every extra pillow on the floor; Betty was carrying two of her own, most likely what Bewly really had his eyes on.

Whatever happened, you could not stay mad at this group for long; it was almost impossible. By the time Monday rolled around, it was situation normal. Even Viken happened to walk by and, peeking into Sherwin's office for the first time since the promotion, fired a bullet: "Interesting color?"

"Oh thanks, my wife picked it out, its mauve." And mauve it would remain.

Through the fog of Monday morning, we were still humming.

Moonlight Becomes You
And I want you to know
I'ts not just because there's moonlight
Although moonlight becomes you so!

FIVE

Travel and Expenditures

Strategically situated to the lower right of the signature line on the Friday's Expense Report was the question, "Was the expenditure worth it?" We all felt that if we took ownership in what we did, we could stay on budget. For the most part, this was the case.

Fortunately for us, we were the recipient of a great deal of entertaining on the road. The five of us could not wait until March rolled around every year as we knew that the call would be coming from The Debartolo Corporation's headquarters in Youngstown, Ohio for the Festa de Concorso. The famed shopping center developer invited retailers from all over the country to join them for a weekend at The Innisbrook Resort in Tarpon Springs. Reaching into one's wallet was forbidden; all expenses were taken care of. As soon as our Town Cars passed through the gates, everything was on Mr. Debartolo.

There were only two real opportunities in which to incur expenses. The first was a Friday evening stop at Maxwell's, a popular hangout just down the road on Highway 19, and the second was the Waffle House. We never bothered to check into our rooms until the mission to Maxwell's was complete, which sometimes meant rousting the security people at the resort to bring our room keys. It was at Maxwell's that we would extend invitations to any interested members of the opposite sex for an all-expenses-paid, weekend stay at one of the detached villas at Innisbrook. We had a modicum of success selling this package, including one repeat guest.

It truly was an out of body experience watching Claus in action. There was little question in my mind that he was one of those people born a "happy baby." If you can remember the actor Chad Everett in the television series Medical Center, he could be Chad's double. Caparisoned in a classic four gold button, blue blazer from Culwell & Sons, Claus's ice-breaking move was to wear his penny loafers on backwards, the left shoe on the right foot and vice versa. Invariably, he would get the ladies to stare at his feet. It was incredibly effective and hilarious to watch. He would not stop there as the four of us knew what was coming next, and boy could we play along with the script. When queried about his occupation, he would respond, "Oh, I'm a thoracic surgeon from Dallas and am in town to open up my best friend Warren. We were roommates in college." Women would melt like butter as he continued on with this sympathy gathering charade. "His condition is such that I am afraid that he's not going to make it," he would recount in the most sincerest of Texas accents. No matter how many times we became witness to this folly, we could just barely hold it together it was so funny.

Before any of us set out on the road, much like a newly sworn-in Police Officer receives his weapon as standard issue, each one of us received a Friday's Red Card and we were soon to find out that the card was just as lethal. This was a charge card for Food and Beverage, and for the purposes of our group, they could have left out the food. The first $150 charged during any given month was on the house, and the overages were billed at a 50% discount and deducted from your paycheck. The pile of receipts that we five generated during this period could close down a landfill from overcapacity. Bewly, the clubhouse leader in paycheck deductions, could burn up his minimum within an hour's time should there be woman (dollies, as he would refer to them) in his presence, and that was almost all of the time.

A very funny story with Red Card implications in what now has been dubbed The CHiPs Story (California Highway Patrol), has been recanted tirelessly over the years. Blaze and Claus had been entertaining a group of developers at Friday's in Torrance. Blaze made the command decision that he was better suited to captain the Town Car to their hotel in Long Beach. The straight shot down the 405 normally would not have posed any difficulties, but a quite noticeable and sudden lane change by Captain Blaze attracted the attention of two motorcycle officers. It was quickly determined that Blaze should be field tested, so out of the car he went. The officer asked for the L.A. version of a Sobriety Test.

"Kindly recite the alphabet, starting with the letter K." Any one of us, including Blaze, would have had to start singing The Alphabet Song in order to get going on the correct path. A-B-C-D-E-F-G-H-I-J-K, now we're ready for the officer! From the open driver side window, Claus could hear poor Blaze in a low murmur start the tune and buckled over in a fit of laughter. From how Blaze describes it, Claus was having convulsions. Officer #2, by now pretty much agitated by his actions, dismounted from his bike and peered in from the driver's side window. Looking in on Claus, he asked if he had been drinking. Claus, thinking that he had passenger-side immunity, confidently answered, "Yes, of course I have, officer."

It was at the moment when asked how much that Claus removed the Red Card receipt—totaling $486—from his coat pocket and handed it to the officer. Claus, sensing that he was having difficulty coming up with a final tally, volunteered that he had been drinking Johnnie Walker Black and that they were

$4.50 a piece. After a quick calculation, "Sir, that's over 100 drinks." Claus with receipt in hand, "but officer, that was hours ago. Here is a more recent one totaling $130." The officer had to think that scotch alone could not have possibly brought this person to such a euphoric state, and instructed Claus to remove their luggage and briefcases that were stowed on the back seat.

Claus asked, "Oh, do you mean our business satchels, officer?" At that very moment, several empty beer cans were no longer concealed from view. Claus once again, "Oh, don't worry officer, those are the empties." The saga concluded when Blaze was issued a passing grade, and off into the night they went!

Betty could pretty much clear her decks by the time Monday afternoon rolled around, as the four of us were on our way to D.F.W. and would not return until the following week. Expense Reports were submitted on Monday mornings, a most critical time in the life of a business traveler. Staying ahead of what we called "the float," or, more appropriately, staying afloat was the real challenge month in and month out.

All expenses were charged to your personal American Express Card and reimbursed by the company upon approval of your expense report, hence the creation of the float. We all filled out our own reports and when complete checked the math in both directions, stapled the many receipts to the report, customarily trying our best to conceal "receipts in question," signed them, and placed the reports on Betty's desk, winking at her in the process.

It did not take her long to figure out the importance of this task, and to lend an assist, the four of us kept her distractions to a minimum. She would look them over for mathematical errors, of which there were a few. If she did not come in to see you, then you knew the report was going to Sherwin for signature. The four of us would then sweat it out. On occasion, Blaze would send Claus into Sherwin's office to see what he was doing with those reports, at times when another flight out of town was imminent.

In the end, it was always a welcome sight to see Betty heading down to accounting with all four reports in tow.

My favorite expense report story of all time, and there is no surprise that it involved Sherwin and Bewly, took place during our second visit to The ICSC convention in Las Vegas. The Show, as it is often called, is an annual gathering of 30,000 of your closest friends in the shopping center industry. In reality, it was a host of mall owners showing off their properties to prospective tenants, all of whom meet and communicate regularly during the course of the year. For us, it was a given that it was pretty much a waste of time, but Sherwin had an idea and proposed that we discuss the matter over cocktails at Dovie's, a quiet restaurant and bar located next to Midway and the former homestead of Audie Murphy, the legendary WWII war hero.

Sherwin knew that the development schedule was in terrific shape, allowing us some breathing room, and that we were to be rewarded for going "incident free" for some time now. As a bonus, he thought we might all go back out to the ICSC in Las Vegas. It was silly of Sherwin to ask us if we wanted to go. Of course we wanted to go. His elementary style of management could be funny. There were two conditions levied upon us: 1. The Sands will be our home for three days, so let's stay on campus and 2. Keep the expenses down, be reasonable. We were all wondering,"Does he not remember who got him here in the first place?" But, nodding in agreement, off we went. Another surprise was in store: we would be riding out on Triple Six-Whiskey Whiskey.

The bungalows at The Sands were all named after Race Tracks. Bewly, Blaze, and I had rooms in The Aqueduct, and Sherwin and Claus had rooms in the main tower. The Rat Pack made The Sands their home while in Vegas, a perfect hideaway for Sinatra's cronies. Although it fronted on the strip, it was not imposing. The property was much deeper than its width, which contributed to its intimacy. Years later, we learned that Rat Pack had use of a private bungalow tucked conspicuously at the very back of the property with its own unattached garage. Frank always had a Jaguar at his disposal. Every person who has visited Vegas more than once will tell you it is a 48 hour town. We were going to be here for 72 hours under home confinement. Would we become "trip goofy?" Would one of us try to escape?

We hung around the pool for the first two days. Two golfing buddies from Dallas, Preston Hollow and Ben Springer, were the only familiar faces at the hotel. Both fine gentlemen were involved in the development of shopping centers in The Metroplex and would eventually join our landlord roster. Preston, a member of Ballsownly Golf Club, an exclusive male bastion in Far North Dallas, was out here for more fun than work, rebounding from a contentious break-up with his longtime girlfriend, Courtesy Flush, whom he had met while attending college at Southern Methodist.

Springer, on the other hand, had been playing the field in Dallas, selecting brunettes as his primary target. On or around the third or fourth date, Springer would schedule a "shake down cruise" to a San Francisco B & B called The Archbishop's Mansion. The purpose of the weekend was to see if she traveled well. As Springer held these tryouts, we would see perhaps a 20% success rate, with about 1 out of 5 girl's photos making it to his refrigerator door at the bachelor pad, indicating that things with her might actually go somewhere.

Springer, like us was avoiding the convention floor like the plague and had invited retailers to visit both himself and Preston at their suite at The Sands. Preston was enjoying the company of this whacko five-some as it became a form of therapy for him. He even invited Sherwin to play some tennis. Sherwin, not properly equipped nor in any kind of shape for that matter, bought tennis shoes and related gear at the pro-shop. Claus poolside yelled in his direction "Sherwin, who do you think should be next in line for your job in case you drop dead on the tennis court?"

Our final evening having arrived, we were starting to separate and the unit was dispersing. Sherwin phoned my room asking me to meet him at the bar and bring the boys with me. They were nowhere to be found so I went alone. Sherwin had a large snifter of Scotch in front of him packed with ice to the very top of the glass. A perfect way to go should you ask for a refill. Sherwin broke radio silence. "How about if you and I get out of here and see a show. I wouldn't mind seeing Diana Ross over at Caesar's. That would be breaking the rules, ah...what the hell, let's get out of here!" Diana's Motown career was on the wane, but we went anyway. Sherwin bootlegged his refill of jet fuel out the door for the short cab ride over to Caesar's. Sherwin sat at the very edge of the row, a good move considering his full tank of scotch.

It was one of those shows where both audience and entertainer were flatter than a pancake. It was like there was a bad connection. Next, some sporadic heckling; the natives were getting restless. Sherwin was murmuring a boo as if checking his lung capacity for the audition to come. Diana ended the show on a limp note, certainly not the crescendo of old and received a smattering of applause that ended abruptly, leaving the room in wake-like silence. She fired off a critical remark for everyone to hear as if to say to herself, "I'll go to down in flames before I allow this to happen."

Sherwin, as if he was in the opposing huddle and new what play was about to be called, fired back: "Why don't you go home and mow my lawn." My, my, Sherwin had come out of the closet as, surely, that was a side of him that we had never seen before. It took all of three seconds for Security to descend upon our location. Sherwin now flanked by two behemoths with girths so wide that, should they be wearing white shirts, you could see "Gone with the Wind" on their backs, was being shown the door.

For the most part he was a model palace prisoner, pretending that he was just walking out with everyone else. He must have been saying to himself, "What if I see someone I know and they want to stop and chat. What then?" In fact, that happened on more than one occasion. "Sherwin, I didn't realize you were at the show" and "Where are you headed?" How about out the door! Sherwin sank into the backseat of our cab as we sped off to The Sands.

Off in the distance, Bewly, Claus, Blaze, and Springer were standing at a crap table. On my way! Preston, whose status as a Whale afforded him generous comps, preferred Black Jack and was stationed at a roped off table close by. Asking about Sherwin, I told them I was the sure the tennis had to have worn the crap out of him, the heat and all. Springer reported that the table was choppy as the five of us settled in at our position in centerfield. Very seldom would you see a woman at the dice table, as historically it has always been perceived as a rude and crude game of chance. As soon as the stick man pushed the bones in my direction, a middle aged woman with movie star looks pitched camp at the opposite end of the table.

You could almost hear Frank belting out "Luck be a lady tonight" as her male companion filled her tray with $100 chips. Frank continued in my head, "A lady doesn't wander all over the room and blow on another guy's dice." She peered down at the lot of us, maybe thinking we were five handsome devils that she might have fun with. She leaned ever so slowly over the table knowing full well that these horny bastards were going to get a bird's eye view of a pair of jugs that in Claus' words "were delivered straight down from the heavens." The site of them hanging out of her dress rendered Bewly speechless. Not

Springer, who commanded, "Ok, Ryan, roll 'em at the tits." Seven a winner, pass line winner! Shaking the dice waiting for the go ahead, and "What'd you say Springer, roll 'em where?" Chips were flying in every direction as the table action reached a frenzied pace. Even Bewly broke his silence, "Come on Ryan, keep 'em at the tits." Yo eleven, winner! Boy that was fun!

Springer and I found the saloon and Bewly, Claus, and Blaze went in search of more entertainment. The next day's rendezvous point was pre-determined: The Reception Desk at noon where we could all check out together. It was 2:30a.m. when I decided to head back to my room, one of the few times with a pocket full of chips. My room was two doors past Bewly's, so as I turned the corner I could not help but notice the covered dishes neatly stacked to the under side of his door knob. Curious as to what was going on, I pressed my ear to the door, at the same time removing the metal cover from the top revealing Moo Goo Gai Pan, Bewly's favorite dish! Not bothering with utensils, I dove in. As any good sonar man would do, I patiently waited for any sound. Not an easy task when you are foraging for food in a poorly lit hallway, dealing with metal tin upon metal tin.

Suddenly, I heard a voice that was unmistakably Blaze's, and then another, oops a female, then Bewly. Ok, I thought, let's see if we can't join the party. First the gentle knock, "Bewly, it's me Ryan, open up." "Go away we're busy."

Now the begging began, "Come on, I just want to watch, please may I."

Now Blaze, "Go to you room and wait for our call."

"Oh sure, how long will that be?" Next, I laid on the guilt trip "Haven't I been good to you guys?" They thought I might go away by giving me the silent treatment. Perhaps they were right, but I would not go quietly. In the dimly lit hall, I began my John Phillip Souza imitation by marching in place, using the metal dish covers as symbols, loud enough so one could march to its cadence from anywhere in the hotel.

It worked, Blaze cracked the door. "Bring in the food and go sit in the corner."

The room was somewhat dark but not pitch black as light seeped through the partially closed bathroom door affording me a clear picture of what was taking place. There was a naked threesome, that was obvious. The amorous couple of Bewly and his mystery companion clearly were trying to catch their breath during this intermission. Bewly relied on his youth to overcome his deficiencies of a poor diet and lack of exercise.

"Ok, you two, let's get started again. Bewly, roll over and get back on top." Blaze grabbed the back of Bewly's ankles that were protruding off the end of the bed and proceeded to perform what he referred to as the wheel barrel fuck. Bewly's motionless body was rocked back and forth, causing quite a reaction from our mystery guest. Blaze, taking one step forward and then another step back was working up quite a sweat, and quite a boner.

"Bewly, are you any closer to blowing your load?"

"Not really, can you go any faster?"

Snorting Moo Goo Gai Pan through my nostrils—from laughing so hard, Blaze, never one to stop with my training, turned to me and said, "Watch how I am doing this Ryan, cause you will be on ankle duty as soon as Bewly is done."

The next morning, the four of us assembled back in Bewly's room for a debriefing. Preston and Springer were on their way as well. There was no mention of Sherwin's folly over at Caesar's. Blaze intimated that he would like a glass of Chivas, and the excuse that we may never be back worked for Claus. Bewly, deprived of his room service order of a few hours ago, instructed Claus to call room service. Claus dialed it up and in his best Charles Nelson Reilly begins the order: "Hello Room Service: this is Mr.

Bewlinsky's room, you know Bewly! Would you please bring us a bottle of Chivas and English muffins for six. Yes, one bottle of Chivas and ice of course, thank you so much, ta ta now." Click. It's now official, we are all trip goofy! Scotch and Muffins, what a combination. Load up on the strawberry jam!

Right on cue, everyone assembled at Reception and took up positions in one of three check-out lines. Sherwin was focused on getting out in one piece—but first there was some accounting to tend to. It was Bewly's turn at the counter, and Sherwin had an opportunity to witness this as he is standing one line over. "Any charges to your room this morning Mr.Bewlinsky?"

"Yes, we had two deliveries, one around 3a.m., the other more recent, the bottle of Chivas and a few muffins." Bewly's hushed tones were almost inaudible to the clerk as he peeked over his shoulder to see if Sherwin was paying any attention. The printers that spit the bills out were perched on top of a credenza along the back wall. She hit the total button sending the printer needle into a violent back and forth motion as page after page came spitting out. It became fruitless to stay up with the out flow, so the clerk waited until the connected pages folded as they reached the floor. We knew Sherwin wanted to yell STOP as the dah-ding, dah-ding continued. Fortunately for us, we brought the half-empty bottle of Chivas with us for the plane ride home, and after a hefty dose, Sherwin was back to his normal self.

SIX

Telling The Story in Albany

It was Dalton Scruggs, the person responsible for laying the groundwork for Friday's early development, who stressed the importance of telling the story. During my first visit with Dalton, I sat and listened as he spoke to me about the company.

"In 1974, I was in Miami on a restaurant location site trip for T.G.I.Fridays. I was staying at a small 32-room hotel in Coconut Grove named The Mariner, which no longer exists. I was having dinner in their small restaurant, enjoying a glass of wine and looking at the menu when I noticed a gentleman at the table next to me having what appeared to be potato skins. Since I love the skin of a potato with butter and salt, I was quite curious. I walked over and asked this man what he was having. He replied, 'Fried potato skins and they are fabulous.' Needless to say, I ordered them and *they were fabulous*.

"When I got back to Dallas I asked our corporate chef, Finbar O'Sullivan, to hop on a plane, fly to Miami, and experience the 'fried potato skin' first hand. The chef at the Mariner restaurant was very willing to show Finbar exactly how he made them. He came back to Dallas just as enthusiastic as I was about this new appetizer.

"Finbar worked on the production for several weeks to make sure that the end product was crispy and not soggy. Soon after, we put the potato skins on our menu in our Dallas store. A basket had six halves and was priced at $1.95. Because there was a lot of prep time involved before the frying, we prepared about 75 whole potatoes the first day, which made about 25 orders. By 12:30p.m. they were all gone. The next day we prepared 50 orders. These were sold out by 12:15p.m.

"Obviously, word of mouth travelled fast that first day. The following day we baked all the potatoes we could with our limited oven capacity. This was approximately 75 orders. Again, we were sold out by 12:15p.m. At this point, we started raising the price. First we raised the price to $2.45, then again to $2.95, then $3.45, then $3.95 and finally $4.25 per order. The price increases had little effect on the demand for the skins, we were generally sold out every day by 12:30 p.m. Needless to say, we introduced the fried potato skin to all of our restaurants as fast as we could and they were a sensation in all our stores. We had to increase our oven capacity in all stores to help meet the demand.

"Sometime during the first year one of our employees invented a superior scooper that resembled a wire hoop. This greatly reduced labor costs and increased the consistency of the amount of potato left in the skin. Over the next 3-4 years, we introduced numerous variations of the original potato skins. These included Loaded Skins with 1/4 pound of cheddar cheese and crumbled bacon, Mexi-Skins loaded with a Mexican filling with melted cheddar and Monterrey Jack cheese on the top, and Crab-Skin loaded with Crab Mornay.

"In 1979, we spent a great deal of time in Idaho with several top potato producers, trying to develop a mass-produced scooped-out skin on the assembly line that we in turn could convert into one of our potato skins, but we never could get the quality that we needed and eventually gave up on this idea.

"In 1980, T.G.I.F. bought approximately 11,000 tons (or 22 million pounds) of potatoes to make potato skins. These skins were the top selling item at Fridays by a multiple of 400%."

Finishing the story, Dalton continued "Jeff, every one of us will have their own individual style as to how we present the company to the outside world. There are no shortcuts to the process. Do not fall into the trap and assume that the person or persons to whom you are speaking knows all about us. They don't. Approach this task as if everyone you speak to has never heard of Friday's. First and foremost, tell the story before you lose the opportunity to do so. Allow me to use this time together as an example. Imagine you have just walked in to my office as Jeff Ryan from T.G.I.Friday's to meet with me, Dalton Scruggs, from X.Y.Z. Development in Boston. My office happens to be six blocks from your Newbury Street location. Are you going to assume that because you have operated in The Back Bay for several years now that I should know everything about your company? Will you decide that I'll just figure it out? Are you assuming that I have been in your restaurant? Have I tested the food—sampled the menu? Developers are not going to give you all day. By now, I might have spread out a plan of a mixed-use development in the northern suburbs and pointed out a secondary location that is tucked into an office building with virtually no parking. I might tell you it's a great market for Friday's and we can deliver the shell that fall, that the space is renting for $30 a square foot, triple net." He paused. "So, does Friday's sign the lease? Or are they still wondering. 'You guys are owned by Steak and Ale from Dallas right?' or 'Who came first, Bennigan's or Friday's? Doesn't matter, my secretary says that they are pretty similar to one another.' Jeff, I'm telling you, you would expect this to happen back when we had seven locations, however, now that there are 42 it is even more prevalent. So now, Mr. Real Estate person from Friday's, you are sitting there wishing you could go outside and start all over again."

Dalton then used a basketball analogy, again with a Boston twist. "Jeff, I am a huge Larry Bird fan. Do you remember Toby

Gillis from Notre Dame, a fine player in his own right and drafted by the New York Knicks?"

"Of course I do; wasn't he a #1 pick?" I asked.

"May have been. Well a sportscaster asked him if he remembered the first time he heard Larry trash talk on the court. Toby said he remembered the occasion quite vividly. It was his rookie year and the game was at The Boston Garden. Larry was coming off a Cedric Maxwell pick and as Toby switched off to cover Larry, he made a desperation attempt at a block, but his shot had already left his hands. Larry knew it was going in and started backpedaling and as he was doing so, looked at Toby and said "too late." The difference between Larry's backpedaling and ours? He had already taken his shot, but we haven't. You have to take the shot as soon as you can. Jeff, let's reverse rolls. You are now Jeff Ryan from X.Y.Z. Development from Boston. I have been waiting for you in your conference room. Here you come." He was ready to act it out.

"Good afternoon, Dalton is it? Jeff Ryan from X.Y.Z.; pleasure to meet you. Please sit down. Can we get you anything?"

"No thank you, I am fine [do not stop]... Mr. Ryan thank you for taking the time to meet with us. Allow me to spend a few moments of your time to tell you about our company."

Launch into it from there.

"Friday's had its beginnings, in New York City in 1965 when Rev Lawn, a perfume salesman bought a tavern at the corner of First Ave. and 63rd St. on Manhattan's Upper Eastside. Rev's new venture named T.G.I.Friday's featured a shotgun bar, an eclectic turn of the century decor of Tiffany Lamps, red and white striped table cloths, hardwood floors and brass rails. The inside cover of a Friday's match book had enough blank lines to accommodate: Date we met at Friday's, name, address, and phone number, and most importantly a comment line. Heightened by the advent of the birth control pill, Friday's vaulted on the scene as the hottest singles bar in America. The success of which spawned the first franchise location in Memphis, Tennessee in 1970. It was there at a luncheon meeting that Viken Dane and Dalton Scruggs [me] took notice of a packed restaurant with less than stellar service, not to mention an exterior painted a gaudy blue. Viken and I, back then executives for a corrugated box company in Nampa, Idaho were in town attending a sales meeting. They decided right then and there to table an investment in a struggling Duck Farm in nearby Brinkley, Arkansas and seek out Rev Lawn in New York City. The result of their meeting was a newly formed franchise group with the rights to seven cities. During one of these follow up visits to New York they both stepped into Maxwell Plum's, another highly successful but much larger restaurant and bar on First Avenue. Warner LeRoy, owner of Maxwell Plum's granted permission for the partners to come in and measure the facility—a process that took three days to complete. Imitation being the best form of flattery, elements of the four sided bar were incorporated into the first ever redesign of the Friday's concept.

One new design element—not taken from New York—became an overnight sensation, The Multi-Level Phone booth. Female customers clad in mini-skirts made their way to the phone on the top level, and guys scurried into the phone booth below. Needless to say, the revenues from this activity—in slot machine parlance Coin In—were prolific.

It was decided by the four (two Holiday Inn executives joined the fray) members of the newly formed group to launch their first restaurant in Old Towne Shopping Center on Greenville Avenue and within close proximity to The Village, a massive apartment complex with 36 swimming pools. Friday's opened in January of 1972 to a rousing success.

Interestingly enough, we borrowed the money ($100,000) to build the restaurant from Old Towne Village Bank. Each one of us putting up $10,000 to secure the loan. The total cost to build that Friday's was $160,000. Within the first three months, the contractors were paid the remaining balance from the cash flow of the restaurant. Little did we know that this would become the "Capitalization Story for the Ages." The partners never had to inject another dime of our own equity into the venture.

Soon after the franchise merged with Rev to form T.G.I.Friday's, Inc. Today there are over 40 T.G.I.Friday's coast to coast. Our Average Unit Volumes are the highest in the industry. An average of over 5000 customers walk into a Friday's on any given week. Everything on our menu is made from scratch, salad dressings, soups, sauces, everything with the exception of our Cheesecake which is specially made and flown in from New York. We will change our menu twice a year and sometimes more, and our Food and Beverage sales are a respective 65% to 35%. We build our restaurants with materials that age well; oak floors, brass rails, authentic glass lamps, authentic tin ceilings and high quality tile. Our restaurants that are ten years old look better than the new ones, because they have had an opportunity to age.

Dalton stopped at this point. "So, Jeff, we have now dispelled any thought of innuendos, our friend the developer is not going to bother talking about a space in the back of the project, rather now his focus is on where we will be best suited for the long haul."

"Last but not least, there are two other important reasons why we tell the story not the least of which is the economics of our deal. You're going to ask for a very tall order from a company like X.Y.Z., in the form of a sizable loan, and they need to be totally sold on our company before they agree to it. And, of course, there'll be many dealings with the cities and towns regarding liquor license hearings and planning and zoning. The ability to tell the story effectively will come in handy.

"Good luck up there. I lost a lot of sleep making that Newbury Street location happen. In the beginning we were not sure if we were going to be able to call it T.G.I.Friday's or just Friday's even. The powerful neighborhood associations perceived us as that 'singles bar' from New York City. In their defense, they really didn't have much to go on as that was our first east coast venture. If by chance one of the members saw us at The Prado in Atlanta or at Keystone Crossing in Indianapolis then they may have garnered some support, but even then who knows. The bottom line is that we settled on Exeter Street Friday's until we could prove to them that we were going to be worthwhile neighbors. It was a win win. Hell, what do you bet the folks that live outside of Beantown look at us as that singles bar? You've seen the waiting lines on the sidewalk? Mostly young people at night."

"Not to bore you with stories Dalton, but one summer during my senior year in high school I worked for a company called Newbury Realty. They owned several properties on the street. Anyway, they hired me to paint their fire escapes along the back alley. At that time, the Boston Strangler was still on the loose. Remember that?"

"Oh yeah. They made a movie; Jeff Tony Curtis played the part."

"The women living in those buildings must have reported me to the police as one day they came racing down the alley, siren blaring and all. If memory serves me correctly, their address was 129 Newbury Street. Friday's is at the corner of Exeter, so we were closer to Arlington. You do realize, Dalton, that the streets that cross Newbury are in alphabetical order?"

"No, I didn't know that actually."

"Arlington, Bedford, Clarendon, Dartmouth, Exeter, Fairfield, Gloucester, Hereford. The names are from British Royalty, I'm told."

"Was there a reason? I mean for the order? Certainly couldn't be by happenstance?"

"Not sure, Dalton but the cabbies like it. According to one driver, it helps them unscramble the unwieldiness of the city streets."

"Sounds to me like an interesting profession. Fire Escape Painter. Probably the same woman that called the cops on you opposed our application."

"It wouldn't surprise me Dalton."

"There'll be opposition. It just goes with the territory. Oddly enough sometimes all that kicking and screaming is their way of saying that a Friday's would do great here."

"Listen, thanks for your advice."

"You're very welcome. Let's hope it comes in handy. One last thing, Jeff, that session that you and I just did with X.Y.Z.? Let's get the guys together and conduct mock negotiations using our Letter of Intent format as a guideline."

From that meeting came this new activity, a new way to strengthen our presentation skills and practice battling back and forth on deals points. Sherwin filmed the sessions and played back the tape. We had some fun playing back the tape over and over again until he was satisfied that we all had our facts straight. If you feel the need to be brought down to earth, try it sometime. Dalton was right, each one of us would do it differently all the while driving the message home. Bewly for example would take a slide show on the road, often calling ahead to a developer's secretary to insure that there was a projector handy. Blaze scripted his presentation in notebook form. Claus substituted the lyrics of *Moonlight Becomes You* and sang the story. (Just kidding.) As for me, I enjoyed narrating, and, of course, embellishing every chance I got, and adding key facts while distributing menus.

Most of the time, it was about telling the Friday's story to developers, but some of the time it was about being in the right place at the right time and finding the right person to listen. The story came in handy for those times as well, and it was an important skill that we learned to perfect, to be able to tell the story in a conference room or on a bar stool. Our trip to Albany is a demonstration of that type of encounter, transformed into a huge opportunity for Friday's by our instinct to tell the story.

How did we get wind of this site opportunity before anybody else? Perhaps we all have Sherwin to thank for this one! Our first order of business had been to fly in and figure out the puzzle of the inter-related cities of Albany-Schenectady and Troy, not an easy task.

There was a two or three mile stretch of Wolf Road that dissected the triangular shape of Albany's Metroland, which became our area of focus. However, as so often happens in our attempt to penetrate a market with limited site opportunities, one can end up with blinders on. The Pyramid Companies, a highly successful upstate New York shopping center developer, was building Crossgates Mall, a retail project of gargantuan scale delayed ten years by environmental groups protesting the threatened habitat of a rare migratory butterfly, The Karner Blue. Meanwhile, Kamm Charge, the company's founder, could not get together with us on "the numbers." Not all too surprising during this period.

Sherwin, desperately needing to get up to speed with both Blaze and me, flew into Albany for a brief overnight stay. At the time of his arrival, there were no specific sites to show him, but we figured he would at least get a chance to see what we are up against. So far, we were batting 0 for 4 here and there wasn't any reason to believe that we would drop to 0 for 5 by noon the next day. At least that is what we thought!

After a brief check-in at The Americana Hotel, we decided to begin our Happy Hour tour at Park V, a popular restaurant and bar located across the street. Sherwin, having been cooped up in Dallas, was bubbling over with enthusiasm and chatting up a storm. The road was fun, especially the first two nights out of the gate. We situated ourselves at the bar in close enough proximity to instigate a conversation with a lone and very attractive woman. Little did the both of us know how propitious of an encounter this would be with Helen Troy, a charming public relations consultant with strong ties in Albany. 'Why not let Sherwin run with this conversation,' I thought. 'It would be good for his psyche.'

Sherwin, with a fresh order of drinks on the way, proudly volunteered that we worked for Friday's Real Estate and were in town looking for a location.

"Have you had any luck?" Helen asked.

"No, but we'd sure like to be here," said Sherwin. Almost instantaneously, Helen suggested that I contact, Hudson Squire, a bachelor friend and owner of Stuyvesant Plaza on Western Avenue in The Town of Guilderland. She described where he was located, and scribbled his name on a drink napkin and handed it to me. (Why didn't she hand it to Sherwin? Aha, he was wearing a wedding ring, maybe that's why?)

How many numbers have you lost in this manner? The dreaded crumpled napkin. Great name for a Piano Bar, right? 'Nice gal, where did you meet her?' 'Oh, we met at The Crumpled Napkin.' Don't you find it incredible, myself included, the distance a guy will go to recover a lost or mangled number? In the case of Ben Springer, who lost a number altogether while on a trip to Chicago, the gesture was all the more incredible. He wanted to find this girl so bad that he actually had the Chicago phone book mailed to him so he could attempt to find her. I don't think he succeeded, but that would have been one hell of a story to tell the kids.

Sherwin held court over dinner, all the while doing an excellent job of questioning Helen about the Albany market. 'This guest lecturer stuff is great,' I reflected. 'She is making my job of educating Sherwin a lot easier.' After dinner, he faded fast and bade us a good evening. Helen, with a gleam in her eye, came right out and suggested that I follow her home for a nightcap, a short two-exit ride on the Adirondack Northway. The journey was going smoothly until she pulled over into the breakdown lane. 'Great time to have second thoughts,' I sat thinking to myself. Instead, she sauntered over to my window, leaned in and, in the same breath as the nibble on my earlobe, whispered "It's probably a good idea that you turn your headlights on."

She took charge as soon as we stepped inside her cozy split ranch. "Make yourself comfortable on the couch." On her way to the bedroom she dimmed all the lights only to emerge seconds later wearing a red negligee. Then there was a ceremonious lighting of candles—red candles of all shapes and sizes—the interior of the house was taking on a sense of macabre.

Her sleek silhouetted figure turned to face me from the threshold of the bedroom door. An extended index finger, the signal to come hither.

Once between the sheets, exploratory probing began in earnest. We were headed for homeplate when my right hand made an interesting discovery—a smooth vaginal surface, a first for me.

Hold on a second. Should I be asking any questions? After all, Helen had more hair on both legs than she did on her snatch. No, no, keep quiet for once in your life! What is the worst that could happen?

Undeterred, and with a bit of naivet`e, I declined to raise an inquiry flag and proceeded with gusto!

The next morning, Helen reminded me to call Hudson. This time—in hindsight, good luck—the napkin was still there.

Sherwin was off to Philly on the early morning flight and asked that I join him and Blaze later that evening. He barely had enough time to ask me about Helen before I told him it was my first experience with a "Bald Eagle." Excitedly, Sherwin said, "You can tell us all about it later. See you in Philly!"

Sherwin was feeling the pressure from the highs and lows of the business. An experienced real estate professional will tell you that one month there may not be enough deals to go around and the next month you are concerned that you may have to delay signing one because there are too many. And it is never permissible to err on the latter; a developer scorned is a developer lost.

Little did we both know that there would be an Albany deal accompanying me to Philly. As luck would have it, Hudson had called our Dallas office and relayed a message to Betty for me to call. He was able to meet me later that day—what a coincidence. Stuyvesant Plaza, and the future home of Friday's, did not attract my attention at first, no question a rookie mistake. Although strategically positioned, it appeared to me to be a decades-old open air shopping center ringed with a series of well kept office buildings. Across the street, Binghamton-based Coco's, had apparently become impatient with the search. They mistakenly converted a former fast food site without securing additional parking sufficent for dinner crowds. Friday's would surely exploit this weakness, sending Coco's on a Bataan-like Death March. And, sure enough, that is what eventually happened.

Driving through The Plaza parking lot on the way to Hudson's office, the only real option that I saw was to tear down a former Ho Jo's restaurant. Fronting Western Avenue, this freestanding site would be ideal. 'This is way too easy,' I thought to myself.

Hudson's perception of Friday's was limited to his visits to New York City and what his friends had told him about our Newbury Street location in Boston. This was an opportune time to bring him up to speed. As the story unfolded, I could sense his eagerness to talk about how and where we could fit Friday's into The Plaza. It seemed he was prepared to move mountains. Ho Jo's footprint could not be expanded, so Hudson suggested that we blow out the end cap across the entranceway affording Friday's the same visibility to Western Avenue. This would work for us as long as we could preserve the existing parking field for the duration of the lease, in other words, establish a no-build area in front of the restaurant.

For any other owner, having a tenant dictate where you can and cannot expand your center would be a major blow to making the deal. Hudson, shrewdly, saw it differently. He knew Friday's was going to become his new anchor tenant.

Hudson finally inquired about the deal. 'Here's my chance, the first time with the training wheels off!' I thought. We proposed that he deliver the shell with all necessary utilities and contribute $1,000,000 towards the cost of construction of our restaurant in exchange for Base Rent that will be the equivalent of 5% of our annual sales, all revolving around a twenty-year term with four five-year options.

Incredibly, after a short pause, Hudson uttered those magic words: "Let's do it."

There were modifications, however, we had the foundation of an agreement which was incorporated into a Letter of Intent and, soon after, Hudson executed a lease in our office on Midway.

Sherwin came back in town for his customary rubber-stamp approval. A walk into a packed Coco's on a wintry evening was all that was required: "This is great, we get in here and no one will be able to chip away at our location!" 'Wow, Sherwin may be picking up a few pointers,' I thought to myself.

Our proposals were often called Build-to-Suits. Essentially, they were long term leases accompanied by a landlord contribution; call it a loan if you will. Drawn down in three construction progress payments, the money was applied towards a General Construction Contract that in 1984 averaged $1,200,000 (not including owner-provided items such as furniture, fixtures, and equipment).

Friday's in-house Architectural and Construction Departments, as professional a group as you could possibly find, would take the project from preliminary site planning all the way to a Certificate of Occupancy. Most General Contractors knew of the high standards by which Friday's conducted business as word traveled, but until they had lived it, forget it.

Friday's took the Six Ps (Proper Planning Prevents Piss Poor Performance) concept to another level. Armed with airtight drawings, veterans like Colt Hammer (from our in-house construction department) were often in the field insuring that there were no shortcuts taken en route to the finish. Colt knew all to well that the G.M. had the final say as to whether or not the job was worthy of turning over to Operations. The final inspection, called the "walk through," was more often than not a highly contentious affair. A G.M., to the chagrin of a first time contractor, would inspect every nook and cranny first and then tend to the obvious. As much as Colt had tried to prepare the G.C. for this day, you could not predict the outcome. On more than one occasion, the 64 foot antique rowing shell, in rowing parlance called The Eight for the eight single oar rowers on board, was left outside the building until it was too late. One G.C. in Philly, realizing that he had clearly blundered, asked if he could saw the shell in half, only to be denied.

So, it was off to Philly, while at the Albany Airport it occurred to me that a friend of mine, a highly respected retail leasing specialist, by the name of Linda Bird, had traveled to Philly on numerous occasions. Perhaps she knew of The Bellevue Hotel and could recommend a restaurant or two. 'Dial her up,' I thought. 'Wait, what is your real motivation for calling her?'

"The Bellevue? You're going to love it. The better rooms

have the number 5 or 7 on the end, so ask for one of those. Check out the Library Bar on the 19th floor, right in your wheelhouse, there is an oil painting on the wall, I believe it is called The Skater, spectacular! Oh and take Sherwin and Blaze to The Saloon if you have time. Nice to hear from you, gotta run!"

A bit tired from the previous evening, the best thing for me to do was hold vigil in the Library Bar until Sherwin and Blaze arrived. Surely they would find their way there. Linda Bird was right. This was the spot. Huge leather chairs to sink into, The Skater looking at your every move within the windowless room, shut out from the hustle and bustle of the city streets below.

Sure enough, Shewin and Blaze stepped off the elevator and with a big shit-eating grin, I removed the Albany Letter of Intent from my coat pocket. "Here, thought you might want to read this."

"God Almighty, Ryan, this is a life saver, how did you pull this off?"

"Let's give the credit to Helen of Troy on this one!" I mused.

The three of us decided to stay right at home and made a night of it. Sherwin kicked back now that the trip had turned productive. Our bartender, by the name of Joey, picked up on Sherwin's Texas accent and appropriately asked about the Cowboys-Eagles rivalry, as this was the weekend that the Eagles were on their way to Dallas to face the Cowboys. Blaze piped in to tell him about a quote from Skip Bayless, the venerable sports scribe from either the *Dallas Morning News* or *The Times Herald*, he couldn't remember which: "The Philly fans are so rough and tough, that when the Eagles are out of town, they go to the airport and boo landings!" Joey got a real kick out of that one.

We lasted right up until last call when the check was brought over. "Give it to Tex," Blaze said to Joey. Sherwin examined it carefully. "I don't want to buy the hotel," he complained modestly. Joey, now heavy on the Philly accent replied, "Whaddaya expect, the Chivas's are $7 per!" ("Per" is Philly-speak for "each.")

Blaze was holding up his end of the bargain as the next morning we got to look at his new site in Bensalem, just outside of Philadelphia. Sherwin thought that we could slot it right after Albany giving us an opportunity to frontload the 1984 schedule with cold weather sites. So far so good. Our Philadelphia City Line location, the first to open in 1981, immediately set in place a rivalry with Boston's Back Bay, much like the Sixers and Celtics or Flyers and Bruins. Both flagship locations, they provided a boost to their suburban counterparts as the hype began to build and word spread of an impending opening. City Line's impact could be felt far across the Delaware River into New Jersey as there were a great many commuters from that side of the river. Blaze and I had already formulated a battle plan for New Jersey; we just hadn't told Sherwin about it.

The rental car was returned without a mishap. We were gaining points with our friends in Risk Management! We all know as frequent travelers that airports are a prime venue for people watching, and this day did not disappoint. Blaze got a jump start as he gestured for us to check out a couple, looking to be in their late 60s, waiting along with several of us for the bus that would ferry us back to the terminal. It was quite obvious that this man's wife, a modern day Norma Desmond, standing front and center, wearing a full length leopard skin coat, the authenticity of which was quite suspect, was in charge. She definitely was wanting of attention. Her husband, no oil painting himself, was sitting on a bench guarding the one piece of luggage in their possession. The oversized bag had all the trade marks of a Louis Vuitton, hand stitched in Nanning maybe, but not in Paris. The bus arrived, prompting everyone to gather their belongings and queue up outside.

Just then we all heard the authoritative order, "Harry, bring the Louis!" Can you imagine?

Albany drew the #1 position in 1984, opening on January 30th. Buddy Busch took advantage of the holiday break and moved his crack Opening Team into position. They were the best of the best that the company had to offer, the Friday's Navy Seals, if you will. To them, this wasn't a job; it was an adventure and a calling.

Buddy had his fingers crossed hoping that his squad, backed up by raw recruits, could hold the line. A few of the new hires came from the ranks of other restaurants, asking themselves what could possibly be different other than the menu and a new uniform. Just focusing on the kitchen alone, it's almost a sure bet that not any one of the many new cooks had any previous experience with handling this level of volume, let alone the number of items on the menu. Friday's knew that the highest number of defectors would come from the ranks of these mercenary types, but it was all part of the weeding-out process. As Major Finchham said to Colonel Ryan in Von Ryan's Express: "I told you, Ryan, if only one gets through, it will be worth it."

One thing was for certain. There would be no respite, as there were two openings scheduled for March.

Cannon to right of them,
Cannon to left of them,
Volley'ed and thundere'd;
Storm'd at with shot and shell,
Boldly they rode and well,
Into the jaws of Death,
Into the mouth of Hell,
Rode the six hundred.

Buddy's crew performed admirably well. That was to be expected, but the telling part was yet to come. The Opening Team Squad Leader may say, "Piss on the fire. Call the dogs in, the hunt is over!" His orders were to pack up and hit the road. We had another to open. How would the restaurant staff—left untethered—handle itself now?

Nobody foresaw what was in store for Albany over the next several months, or years for that matter. It was as if one day the lollygagging stopped. Albany became the Seabiscuit of the company. It was incredible to watch this horse of a restaurant gallop its way into the Winners Circle.

SEVEN

RAMP

Claus had taken a liking to his weekly commute to California splitting his time between L.A. and The Bay Area, perhaps too much so. It was in Laguna Niguel where Claus met a woman to whom he referred only as The Snake Lady. Apparently after their first romantic interlude, he discovered a tattoo in the form of a serpent somewhere on her body. What was it about assigning women pseudonyms? A bachelor friend of ours, Axel Starre, was seeing a woman he called The Phone Company Lady. Axel divulged little only to say that she was single and worked for AT&T We all knew Axel's affinity for large breasts, so you could add that to the list. They quickly fell into a hedonistic routine as every Sunday evening after 60 minutes, Andy Rooney must have been her cue to get ready—Axel would leave his apartment in North Dallas for the ten minute ride to her house. Sans any pleasantries, they would jump into the hay and have their way with each other. If she asked Axel how he would like it, his answer; "Without conversation." Axel would be home before the 10 o'clock news. Only once in the ten years that this arrangement went on did we see them out in public together.

Sherwin did his best to protect Claus, but it was just a matter of time before his lack of production would come into question by others. Clavin gets the credit for that. Prior to his arrival, paper shuffling had always been kept to a minimum. All we had to do was to walk into someone's office to discuss a matter and it was done. Viken did not have as much as an in-basket until the "memo king" showed up. He cc'ed the world with the most pedantic of crap, a forest conservationist's worst nightmare. One had only to look at the Development Schedule, now distributed to every Department at Midway, with the list of sites and their corresponding Real Estate Directors names to know that Claus had only two deals in the pipeline, San Mateo and La Jolla. In retrospect, these two locations would prove to be "home runs" for the company so from that perspective Claus paid for himself, but that was not how it worked. It would take at least 14 months before the company would find out if any one of us was worth the investment in time and money because that's how long it took to get one restaurant open.

Once the gossip mill started to work on Claus, it became difficult to stop. Sherwin found himself in a dilemma. How long could he keep the wolves at bay? He had to know that The Snake Lady was picking Claus up at L.A.X. in her Mercedes convertible as he had not submitted a car rental bill in over 6 months. Even Accounting raised a flag in the beginning. "Claus, you forgot to submit your car rental bill?" "Oh no, brokers are picking me up curbside at L.A.X.!" Claus became the ultimate California Dreamer!

Sherwin must have had something up his sleeve as once again we were asked to meet him for cocktails at Dovies. It was becoming more difficult to keep a straight face at these "out of left field" meetings, particularly at cocktail hour. He informed us that the folks in operations wanted to harvest more booty out of The Bay Area. That was understandable as The Friday's in San Jose, built in 1977, was perennially in the top 10.

In an unprecedented move that Sherwin called R.A.M.P. (for Rapid Advancement Market Penetration), Bewly, Blaze, and I were to accompany Claus to San Francisco for a three day trip in a bold attempt to quickly come up with sites in the coveted markets of Walnut Creek and Mill Valley. Claus always talked about the fact that he could be related to General Blucher whose Prussian troops reinforced Wellington at Waterloo. Perhaps the three of us could perform the same heroics for Claus. Unfortunately, we knew going in that this was a boondoggle of a mission. But, orders will be orders so off we went. The four of us bivouacked at the Andrews Hotel, a charming European style B & B across the street from Trader Vic's. It was here that we decided to divide and conquer. Blaze and I would head east over The Bay Bridge to Walnut Creek, and Bewly and Claus would cross the Golden Gate into Marvelous Marin County.

Once our Town Cars split up, all communication would be lost. All we could do was pick out a rendezvous point and synchronize our watches. Perry's in Mill Valley it was; Happy Hour, be there, book 'em, Danno! Perry's was sitting in the cat bird's seat, in an almost impregnable position. If you could lower our prototype building from a Sikorsky helicopter, you would place it on top of their roof. They were sitting on our 100% location.

Even the map wanted to tell us that we were not welcomed. Mill Valley, small-town California at its best. They looked at us as if we were a colony of African Bees ready to take up shop in one of their pristine canyons. We were not going to be here anytime soon, how about twenty-five years later anytime soon? It became apparent that Walnut Creek's canyon-like setting was not going to yield a site, plain and simple. There are a handful of markets that you are just not going to penetrate, and this was one of them. The good news was, however, that Claus was going to deliver San Mateo later that year.

The bad news was that was going to be the extent of our development in The Bay Area for some time. Sherwin would have to show a little backbone in telling Midway that we had a two store region and that was it, not an easy task for our man behind the desk.

We arrived at Perry's towards the end of Happy Hour only to find Bewly and Claus bellied up to the bar in the company of two rather attractive "Valley Girls" dressed in casual elegance. After a quick chat about the day's futility, Bewly had informed us that this encounter with the girls was a carryover from a late lunch. Blaze, in assessing the situation, pointed towards the city where he thought the two of us may be able to roust out Ursula Blowfish, a Senior Leasing Director for The Coral Fund, our landlords in Hackensack, New Jersey.

Their offices were somewhere in the Financial District. Going against rush-hour traffic, wheelman Blaze made great time back into the city. We slid into Mulherns on Green Street where Blaze called Ursula. "She's on her way," said Blaze in a confident tone as if to say, 'See, I've still got it!' Up until this time, we were wondering how Bewly and Claus were going to make it back over the bridge.

Watching Ursula's entrance into Mulherns put that thought to rest. Blaze's description of her was spot on, a tall statuesque brunette, perfectly coiffed hair and dressed to the nines. She looked ravishing and every Advertising Exec who frequented Mulherns attested to that fact by turning their heads in her direction. There was something about this evening, full moon perhaps or maybe it was just being at a great bar in a great city with the right company. Blaze and Ursula had already broken bread with the New Jersey deal, so there was very little in the way of business to discuss. Perfect, we could expect a freewheeling conversation.

Blaze was married and far from a hound on the road, but he loved to mix it up. Versed on a great many subjects, whenever he sensed a lull in the action, he would reach down into his grab bag of knowledge and throw out a tidbit of information, chumming for someone to run with an interesting subject matter. As much as Claus had Moonlight Becomes You in his repertoire, Blaze, depending upon the level of Chivas, could crank out two stanzas of the epic Oscar Wilde poem, The Ballad of Reading Jaol.

> *Yet each man kills the thing he loves,*
> *By each let this be heard,*
> *Some do it with a bitter look,*
> *Some with a flattering word,*
> *The coward does it with a kiss*
> *The brave man with a sword*

Later in the evening, he would crank out the rest:

> *He did not pass in purple pomp,*
> *Nor ride a moon-white steed,*
> *Three yards of cord and a sliding board*
> *Are all the gallows' need.*

Blaze never finished the last two verses; perhaps they did not have the impact that he was looking for or maybe it was the preventative measures of Chivas working against him. I rather think it is the latter.

The three of us left Mulherns and dined at The Tadich Grill. Ursula perused the wine list with the utmost of impunity, knowing full well that Coral Fund was picking up the tab. "Bring us a bottle of the 1978 Heitz Cab, 'The Martha's Vineyard,' and get it breathing, Oh, and we'll do the pouring."

"I'll bring it straight away," said the waiter. After dinner, Blaze wanted to get the Town Car in the barn and gave me the nod that it was okay to keep Ursula company. One thing was for sure, that it was time to move on, so we made our way to the sidewalk. I had to think fast, otherwise this evening's segment would be over. Ursula was far removed from the pathetic volleying back and forth that you so often hear from couples. "What do you want to do?" "Oh I don't care, what do you want to do?"

Fortuitously, a cab with a nose for a fare, pulled up to the curb. That's when I said to her, "Top of the Mark for a night cap?" She applied a slight tug to the elbow as if to pull me closer and said, "Ryan, you could be dangerous." Apparently that meant yes, as she filed into the backseat on the passenger side. She removed a compact from her purse and began touching up her lipstick.

At the same moment, from my position behind the driver, I leaned forward and rolled a crumbled twenty dollar bill onto his lap. "Top of the Mark, and by the way you're Steve McQueen." The G force tossed Ursula back in her seat, compact flying out of her hands. For the first time that evening, she became speechless, only to hold on for dear life as the four door sedan crash-landed at each intersection on its rapid decent down Powell Street, sparks flying out from underneath the chassis.

We were renacting the chase scene from the 1968 movie, Bullit, only our destination was The Mark Hopkins Hotel. After a couple of Glenny's, it was quite obvious that Ursula had seen enough surprises for one evening. "Check please!"

We took a circuitous but uneventful cab ride back to my hotel. "Ryan, that was fun," she said, as she planted a slight peck on my cheek.

Quietly, I found my way to my room, thinking it had been a full day. No sooner had my head hit the pillow when the phone rang. It was Blaze. "Get dressed and meet me in the lobby in 10 minutes. Claus is in trouble; I'll fill you in on the details on the way." Click. Looking at my watch, it was close to 11. I wondered what kind of shape they would be in.

Blaze glided the Town Car back over the Golden Gate, all

the while telling me that Claus couldn't find Bewly and that the Town Car's battery was dead. Blaze said that Claus sounded a bit incoherent. What a surprise! When we arrived at the scene it was obvious that Claus had enlisted the help of his female companion to assist in jump starting the towncar. The two cars were facing each other and the hoods were open. That was as far as it went. A post mortem had shown that Claus had to have made an improper cable connection as the cable ends had clearly melted onto the battery posts. Telltale sparks had to have told him that something was amiss.

Blaze, as was customary, took charge. "Lose the cables, close the hood and say goodbye to Miss Whomever." Claus, knowing that it may not be a good idea to get any closer to her car than necessary, bid adieu from afar. He gave it the over the shoulder wave from the back window as Blaze steered a southerly course for The Golden Gate Bridge.

Each morning, the hotel staff would prepare a table of fresh coffee, croissants, muffins, fruits, and a small, neatly stacked array of newspapers for every floor to enjoy. It was a wonderful touch. All we had to do was leave our room for a brief moment and mosey a few steps down the corridor. It was the next morning that I peaked out the door and eyed the bounty at the end of the hall. The coast was clear, as I traipsed down the hall with only my boxer shorts on and a dreadful case of bed hair. Pouring myself a cup of java with my back to the hallway, I could hear a door close and then footsteps. So I turned around. Heading towards me was this great looking gal, dressed in a dark blue pinstripe pantsuit, black leather shoulder bag and shoes to match with a walk that was saying, "Look at me, today I am going to open up a fresh can of kick ass."

There was nowhere for me to run and hide, so I engaged. "Good morning, let me be the first to tell you that you look spectacular!" Before she was able to respond Claus cracked his door open, glanced down the hallway and said, "Ryan, ask her if she would like any scotch in her coffee."

Our somewhat speechless guest—with coffee in hand—sauntered off to the elevator, but not before turning back to deliver a quick smile.

Bewly called to say that he was coming into the city during the morning commute. Apparently last evening's conquest worked for a lawyer in the Transamerica Tower. We would inform the car rental agency of the abandoned Town Car while at the airport.

Our trip to California was over, and, as we had anticipated, we had nothing to show for it. The Bay Area would prove a tough market to break into for years to come. Between the car debacle and my weak moves in the hotel hallway, it was high time to get back to Dallas and find some new assignments.

EIGHT

Little Rhody

Dallas-based American Airlines became the east coast carrier of choice. The roots of my loyalty to the brand had been planted long before my years at Friday's. For me, the important moment was a field trip to Logan Airport where as a Boy Scout we were ushered to a gleaming American Airlines 707 with the name The Silver Star inscribed on the fuselage. In my mind, there was no other airline that existed.

For the first six months of 1981, the trips to either Boston's Logan or New York's LaGuardia became pretty much routine. American's frequent flyer rewards program, a stroke of marketing genius, solidified our loyalty to the carrier. The Friday evening return flights left either airport at around 6p.m. and arrived at D.F.W. in time for the four of us to reach our rendezvous point, Friday's at Sakowitz Village. I was usually last to arrive by 9:30p.m. Bewly and Claus would already be there, and Blaze, arriving from Philly, would be just ahead of me.

The equipment that American flew on these routes was the DC-10, the workhorse of the fleet. The standard joke going around about this airplane? What do you get when you cross Billy Jean King with Bo Derek? You guessed right! A DC-10. Generally the Friday evening runs were packed to the rafters. This was back in the day when smoking was permitted, and this aircraft turned into a flying pool hall half-way to the target.

Social gatherings took place in the aft section, and passengers stood by the galley partition much like people congregate in a kitchen at a house party. Several downed cans of cold Bud and a good conversation, and before you know it we are starting our descent over Texarkana.

Mike Hardinballs, just prior to leaving for Costa Rica, was the first to introduce us to the front cabin of this magnificent aircraft as part of an early Christmas gift for myself and Blaze. Unbeknownst to me, there were many more eventful trips to come, up in the seats that we affectionately called The Lazy Boys.

Mike was conducting a year-end whistle stop tour of our progress in the Northeast, the last stop being the Boston market. Before heading over to Logan, the three of us had stopped for a late afternoon lunch at The Salty Dog in Faneuil Hall Marketplace. The productive trip had put Mike in a cheerful holiday mood, though that was about to change as he witnessed for the first time the hundreds of worn out businessmen queued up at Gate 62 for the flight back to Big D. A bit discouraged, he redirected us to The Admirals Club, where Sam and I got comfortable in the lounge. Mike, on the other hand, with the three tickets in hand, went off to pay a visit at the front desk. Moments later we were informed that there had been a change in the seating arrangements. "Boys, Merry Christmas, we are dining in the sky," Hardinballs cheerfully reported after handing each us our new boarding passes.

American was promoting a new configuration of their front cabin seating. After takeoff, the chairs would swivel around to a table in groups of four. Linen tablecloths, vodka in glassware, wine, laughter: a perfect way to spend a Friday evening in the air. After dinner, one of the most festive single deck Black Jack games ever to be held above 35,000 feet would break out. Holding the deal for many nautical miles, we exhausted the resources of our fellow first class mates. The flight attendants, sharing in the spoils, would head to steerage searching for willing participants amongst the proletariat.

One particular late Friday afternoon, it was becoming apparent that my return trip to Dallas may not happen until the next day. I did not allow myself enough time to at a minimum get on airport property, return the car, and take a leisurely stroll to the gate. In fact, I resigned myself to the notion that I would take a cab back to the city, check in to the Copley Marriott and fly out on Saturday afternoon. What the hell is the difference? What, don't want to miss a Friday night with the boys?

We, frequent fliers, think that the car rental bus driver is at fault. Why wouldn't we? He or she is the last step between you and the gate. When you climb aboard, don't you just want to say, "Can we cut the 'Welcome' crap, shut the door and get going!" The drivers know that they are in control, they see you giving that exasperated look at your watch. You can see them smirking and thinking 'No need to rush on this fool's account. He didn't leave himself enough time.'

"Airlines please?" You know that they are going to stop at every terminal... don't bother writing them all down, just shut the door and step on it. After waiting for a straggler with three suit cases to board, the bus starts rolling—at last. Finally, the American terminal I thought 'What the hell... I might have a chance!'

Then suddenly, from a distance it looked as though my favorite airplane was still parked at the gate. With all passengers surely on board, my pace quickened. Out of breath, I reached the gate and was now staring at the name tag of my new best friend, Tale Wind, Gate Agent for American Airlines.

Tale, a calm veteran of such emergencies, gave it the Boston accent: "Tryin to get to Dallas ahwee?"

"Ya, I am sorry. Shit, I should have known better not to give myself enough time."

"Let's see what we gawt he-ah," he says as he feverishly works the keyboard. "What brings you to Boston?"

"Site selection for Friday's. We are looking for suburban locations."

"Love the one in the Back Bay! Lawta action at that bah."

At that moment, I remembered a gift certificate in my pocket that was to go to my sister, a school teacher in the burbs, if and when I could get down to see her.

"How about if we buy you dinner?" I suggested, as I stealthily slipped the certificate inside the ticket jacket with just enough of an exposed margin where he would notice, a signal that I was for real.

"Oh you don't have to do that," he protested, as he pulled the jacket in closer towards him so as to not let any of his fellow gate agents in on this secretive exchange.

As with most business travelers, the sound of that Boarding Pass spitting out from down below was music to my ears and with a wink, Tale tore off the new information and inserted it inside a fresh American ticket jacket.

"See ya next time Mr. Ryan."

"Definitely, I will be back and forth for the next few months anyway."

Peering down at the stub, I noticed Cabin F Seat 3B. Tale had hooked me up with First Class. This was the start of a wonderful relationship for the both of us. For the ensuing return trips from Boston, it got to the point where Tale would look up for me as soon as I made my approach to the gate, only to gesture that he had me covered. Harry Chapin may have written the lyrics this way: "You see Tale would be dining at Friday's and I would be Dining in the Sky! I took off for the footlights and Jeff took off for the sky."

Airline personnel have thankless jobs dealing with selfish travelers day in and day out, but that does not stop them from performing individual acts of kindness that go beyond the call of duty.

On the top of my list is one involving an Eastern Airlines stewardess that came to my rescue. Leaving a Hertz rental car at LaGuardia was painless, all that was required was to drop off the keys at the counter on the way to the gate. Safely back at Logan and now standing beside my Olds Cutlass, it took only seconds to realize that the car key chain in my hand had a Hertz logo. Nice going Ryan. Guess where your keys are? In New York, dumbass! Well, I guess it could happen to anybody, the cars were the same model.

Back to the gate I went. The shuttle departures were every hour on the half hour. But then a better opportunity presented itself. I motioned to a nearby stewardess who clearly was heading back to New York, and asked if she would kindly deliver a set of keys to the Hertz counter and bring my keys back on the return flight. "Wait here," was all that she said! Dangling my keys between thumb and forefinger, she proudly deposited them in the palm of my hand later that afternoon.

Now on days of departure, I leave my keys behind sitting on the top of one of my four tires. Certainly hoping that no one has witnessed this move. Knock on wood, the system has not failed me yet. Though don't get me wrong, there have been minor panic attacks during which I have reached underneath and felt nothing but tire. Try the next wheel well, and there they are!

I was hoping my luck in those high-altitude BlackJack games would translate into winnings for Friday's on the ground in a new market: Rhode Island. My plan was to slip down to "where the mobsters eat the lobsters" on one of my monthly visits to Boston. The trip is an easy fifty minute ride on I-95 South. Knowing that this was unfamiliar territory for Sherwin, any mention of this market this early in the game would be counterproductive.

Flanking each side of the Providence River that spills into Narragansett Bay are the cities and towns of The East Bay and The West Bay, respectively. Once, on a trip with Blaze to Harrisburg, Pennsylvania, we had reached an impasse as to which side of The Susquehanna River, a body of water that literally split the market in half, would best support a Friday's. The geography may have been similar in Rhode Island, where within a thirty minute drive, you would find yourself across the border either in Massachusetts or Connecticut. In addition, there were two very distinct markets in the East Bay and West Bay. Warwick-based T.B.E, Inc. would see to it that The West Bay would become our first choice.

T.B.E (The Bitter End) had developed nursing home projects throughout the state. The company's founders, Digger and Euthanasia Plott, owned a 20-acre gem of a site in Warwick at the northeast corner of Route 2, a heavily traveled north and south retail corridor, and Route 117, the east and west access road that carried vital residential traffic.

Unfamiliar with retail development, they thought it wise to hire an expert consultant named Fausto to spearhead their efforts. We spoke on the phone two or three times, and there was no let up to this guy's enthusiasm. We would often hear superlatives mentioned as a caller described a site opportunity. Stands to reason; a caller is trying to get an audience and seeing is believing. The intent was never to crush anyone, as we were overwhelmed with gratitude over the interest level shown in this concept, but we knew it was best to ask the tough questions early on rather than to delay the inevitable.

"That sounds great, we will certainly take a look," we would often say. And, I should mention, when we said that we would take a look, we meant it. Providing lip service was not part of our deal. We asked tough questions but promised big rewards. We had to know at the outset if there was anything wrong with the site. In other words, all great sites have something wrong with them, so we wanted to make sure we knew what it was in each case. This provocative line of questioning stumped a great many callers and put them on the defensive at times, but they would usually soon discover that we had a purpose and just wanted to make the call as productive as possible, for both ends.

Our development team grew to respect TBE, as we had a keen sense after meeting them in the field that they meant business. They were prepared with answers to all of our questions; this was good since with most developers the process was much more difficult. This deal was almost over before it began. At my suggestion, Euthanasia and Tony hopped in my rental car for the ride to Twin Oaks, a very popular restaurant tucked away in a residential neighborhood of Cranston. It is here that we were to meet Digger for lunch.

Euthanasia was riding shotgun in the front, and Tony was in the back. On a residential street a short distance from our destination, Euthanasia happened to notice Digger in his car driving by us in the opposite direction. I quickly decided to make an abrupt turn to give chase, when suddenly Euthanasia's door swung open. Out she went, holding on for dear life to the car door handle as if she was riding side saddle. Instantly, Fausto vaulted from the back seat and heroically pulled her back in moments before her head was about to hit the pavement. In the end, we managed to catch up with Digger, and we decided to visit Federal Hill, Providence's version of Little Italy (to the non-Italians, Garlic Mountain), for lunch at Camille's.

After our stop on Federal Hill, the small talk ended back at T.B.E.'s office, a converted elementary school two miles from the proposed site and within shouting distance of Warwick City Hall. Numerous photos of Euthanasia with politicos from President Jimmy Carter to the nearby mayor, lined the walls. Fausto stood behind, Euthanasia seated at her ornate desk, Digger relaxed on a leather couch, I laid out the history of Friday's for them.

Euthanasia, the troika's spokesperson, chimed in and asked, "So what's the catch?" Asking for a $1,000,000 order, and that is really what we were doing, was certainly an interesting feeling inside, but, this being my second time, I wasn't nervous and it felt cool. Almost immediately after the numbers rolled off of my tongue, I was looking for a reaction. Our mock training sessions paid huge dividends in this regard.

Our Letter of Intent was the most comprehensive in the industry. We felt that if the business deal was spelled out properly, then there would not be any costly surprises down the road. Past experiences had taught us to spend the time up front to get it right, and for the most part we did. Everything down to soil conditions was important enough to discuss in the early stages. Overlooking seemingly small considerations could land us in big trouble. In Tarrytown, New York, for example, the landlord delivered our pad location as per our agreement, but we soon discovered that the soils beneath the building would not support normal footings. Piles had to be driven 150 feet before we found resiliency, a job costing $100,000 or more at the time. Shame on us that there were not any provisions in our document to place the burden on the landlord for such an occurrence, but we learned from these mistakes. More than likely the developer was keenly aware of this pre-condition. These live and learn situations ensured that we very rarely allowed it to happen a second time.

In Warwick, our bases were pretty much covered, and we were looking forward to the arrival of our new friends in Dallas to ink the lease. We used the home court to our advantage, a total team effort with the primary role of the real estate person to keep the visiting party entertained during the evening. This strategy of "wearing them down at night" worked quite effectively, much like a naval bombardment was an attempt to soften a beachhead, so to was this an attempt at softening the landlord's mental toughness. Our progress during the day was often commensurate with how late we were able to entertain our guests the previous night.

Our in-house legal team sat in waiting, well rested for the long monotonous day ahead, in this case two. Attorney Adam Meiser, brought in for his experience working for landlords, was the spiritual leader of this tenacious three person wrecking crew. His Raid on Entebbe style of negotiating did not win over many landlords; to say the team was thorough was grossly understated. Most of us have heard about Murphy's Law, 'if anything can go wrong it will.' Adam lived by Shultz's Law, "Murphy was a fucking optimist!"

The legal team authored "The Alligator List" for things that could come back to bite us. As Friday's gained experience the list grew. I saw those guys argue over language as trivial as the difference between rat proof containers vs. rat resistant containers. And this wasn't a passing argument; they might even break for lunch over this issue.

One particular landlord left the negotiating table almost in a hyperventilating state he was so upset, only to return after taking in some fresh Texas air.

Our lead guy on the Warwick lease was Hugh Ateitall, a corpulent fellow with Papillon style eye glasses. Although indisputably capable, he was brutally slow and methodical. Come on Hugh, we would often think, the lease is going to expire before it gets signed. The only time he moved with any alacrity was when the test kitchen announced a tasting. He would traipse back to his office, performing a balancing act with the plate of food he so dearly held with his two hands. For him this wasn't a tasting but an ingestion.

The good news about being home was that we could call on the all the support groups that made a project come together. Friday's was ready with the site plan critical to everyone's understanding of the parking field, the folks in construction could query a developer on any outstanding construction issues, and our paralegal, had her finger on the pulse of all liquor license issues, no two applications ever alike.

Scoot Over, our Site Planner, held the most unheralded position in Development, though probably the most important one. The idea was simple: if the site plan doesn't work, then the whole process comes to a screeching halt. We needed to know up front whether or not a site was going to work. Scoot didn't have the luxury of jumping on an airplane and visiting every potential site, so he relied heavily on the information that we provided him. He had to know parking codes, signage restrictions, setback and landscaping requirements, where and how we could place the building as it related to the street.

Could a delivery truck make its way to the back door without taking out a row of cars? Would a car's headlights shine into the dining room? Priority #1 was parking. He paid attention to every detail while flying on VFR. His end product was called The Preliminary Site Plan. This was his domain, and he was indispensable to our team. We spoke to him more than we spoke to Sherwin. Scoot would ask, "Ryan, have you had a chance to peak at the Princeton package that arrived via FedEx. It may be down at reception." I knew it wasn't because FedEx packages were not allowed to linger at the front desk. (Reception was not a mail room, it was Reception.) Scoot would continue, "Buddy is coming out to New Jersey next week to look at the site and wanted to know if you thought it physically might work for us. Let me know if you have any questions." Onto better things: "Are you coming out with us on Thursday night? Bewly wants to check out 8.0, Shannon Wynne's new place at The Quadrangle."

Scoot replied, "I've heard that it's jamming. Why the name 8.0?"

"Eight investors, no experience."

"Cool," Scoot replied. "I'll see if I can get a hall pass from the wife!"

Ken,

additional copies can be purchased on Amazon.but can let me know what you think!

Thanks —

401.529.1772

Negotiations on the Warwick deal were going slower than normal and it was decided that we would wrap things up on a Saturday morning. Everyone was tired; even Euthanasia's patience was wearing thin. The last point of contention was to be the cross hatching of a no build area. Worth noting here is that we were trying to protect our parking field and site lines for as long as we occupied the site, especially important in Warwick because the remaining parcel had yet to be developed. Friday's often became overly territorial on this matter, this time to the point that Euthanasia was at the breaking point. By late morning the next day, she asked if there was anyplace in the office where she could get a stiff drink. Shoe Wagner, a Divisional Vice President whose office along Executive Row was next door to our conference room, happened to be in the office on this Saturday morning. "Shoe, there is a lady in the conference room asking where she can get a drink around here. She's just about had it with this lease bullshit."

"Goddamn Ryan, she isn't going to walk on a deal on a Saturday morning, is she?"

"Not if I can help it."

"I have a stash of Maker's Mark in my desk. Let me bring it down to her, maybe we can diffuse the situation with a little Friday's hospitality."

The combination of the jolt of whiskey and Shoe's charm seemed to soothe Euthanasia's frayed nerves and cajoled her into signing the lease, though not without her getting the last word. Hugh was in his office working on the final draft when she turned to me and said, "Ryan, you've done an admirable job making this deal happen, but I am not going to sign this lease with that asshole (Hugh) in this room."

"Consider it done." This was one of the few concessions that we made during their visit. Hugh holed up in his office, as we couriered the signature pages back and forth to the Conference Room.

We knew that Sherwin would have a great deal of difficulty grasping what we were about to do in Rhode Island. It was understandable for a Texan visiting for the first time. Hell, there were, after all, ranches in Texas larger than the state. Compounding his conundrum was the fact that we were about to throw a spade in the ground on a site that had yet to see any development. The more we drove the farther he crawled into his shell, a telltale sign that he did not know how to broach the subject of telling me that we were out of our minds in considering this site.

In hindsight, every one of us has wished at some time in our life that we had the courage to say "Hey Asshole" the way Reiben (Ed Burns) did in Saving Private Ryan, and if my situation had continued on, the triade may have gone something like this: "Don't you know that I have driven every fucking street, been in every restaurant, some more than once, not to mention the fact that I have lived here and have come back every year for the past ten years to play golf with my pals. This is a great opportunity for us. Now do you get it?" Twenty-five years after the fact, I still sense the frustration of that day.

Well, it just so happens that another chance encounter, this time with someone I knew—Henry Walsh, that saved what was turning into a difficult day. We stopped at Dunkin' Donuts, a popular destination on Route 2 noted for its strong coffee. Henry was just pulling out when he recognized me. He had just returned from a business trip in L.A. and had entertained clients at Friday's in Marina Del Rey. I knew that because he had called my office raving about the place.

Henry rolled down his window as Sherwin and I got out of the car. "Hey, Ryan. We had a great lunch at the Friday's in Marina del Ray. You guys should try to put one here. Henry meet Sherwin Bliss, V.P. of Real Estate for T.G.I.Friday's. This is Sherwin's first visit to Rhode Island."

Henry sure got Sherwin's attention. "How would we do here,

say at the corner of Route 117 and Route 2?" Sherwin asked.

"Oh you mean Euthanasia's property," An absolute out-of-the-park home run!

Well that did it! Sherwin, relieved after hearing a non-partisan vote of confidence, perked up almost immediately and, with coffee in hand, began asking questions like how far we were from Logan and what the Big Blue Bug was all about on 95 in Providence.

"Ryan, how many people live in this state anyway?" he asked me.

"Oh, I believe about a million."

"A million? Hell, Ryan, this waterfront is to die for. What's wrong with this place? They put this shit right on this beautiful harbor." He was pointing to the gaudy pink strip club visible from the highway, the industrial buildings, the decrepit warehouse buildings just taking up space right in this gold mine of waterfront real estate. "Ryan, if we had this kind of setup down in Texas, man, people would jump at the opportunity to develop it."

"Well, Sherwin, you are right. Problem is this place is so small, it's sort of a blessing and a curse."

"Apparently. Hell, Ryan, the King Ranch back home is bigger than this whole state."

"And that's just it," I explained. "Connections are important here. Can't do anything without your mother-in-law knowing about it. So, it's not surprising that they have a hard time putting any decent projects together. These city councils just can't get anything done."

"What a shame, Ryan. Well, maybe it'll get better someday as some of the old-timers pass on. It sure is beautiful here."

"Maybe," I said.

Sherwin kept chirping away all the way to Logan. "So Ryan, what are the women like here in Little Rhody? How about a good story from one of your campaigns as you call them?"

"Come to think of it Sherwin, there is an incredible story involving a Marriott. A waitress from a local golf club met me at my downtown hotel room after work. We had been flirting with each other for a couple of days. On Saturday, I gave her a room key and lo-and-behold she knocks on my door at 2a.m. The room was situated on the first floor mind you. More on that in a minute though. As she started ripping off her clothes she says 'Ryan, when I get done with you, you won't have any bone marrow left.'" Sherwin went ballistic, but I continued. "I get on top, and the moment I make entry she starts screaming like a hyena. Never have you heard anything like this in your entire life. Maybe I am the porn star I dream to be afterall. Moments later, someone is banging on the wall—it has to be the neighbor. No voice, just loud open hand slapping noises but she keeps screaming until we are done, or at least I am done."

Now the festive Sherwin interrupts. "Ryan, do you know why women fake orgasms?"

"No, why?"

"Because they think we care!"

"That's funny! Anyway, after a power nap we get right to it again, and the shrieks were even louder. The next thing I heard was the window crashing behind the drapes. Fuck. 'What was that? Did you hear that?' She replies, 'Hear what?' and that's when I felt it—a hearing aide the size of a hockey puck behind her ear.

Sherwin now buckled over. "A hearing aide? God almighty, what happened next Ryan?"

"Fortunately for the both of us—nothing. After dismounting, I slowly crept over the window only to find a patio stone laying on the floor. Can you imagine? This guy gets out of bed, walks outside, finds something to hurl through the window."

"Do you think he gave it the old discuss throw or an overhead toss?" We agreed that it was probably overhead.

That pit stop at the coffee shop proved to be a fortuitous one for Friday's. Would we have gotten the site approved if Henry wasn't there? As they say in Maine "Hard tellin' not knowin'."

Friday's success in Warwick naturally generated interest from other restaurant companies who wanted to become neighbors on the site, Darden Restaurants being one of the many. The no build provision saw to it that that was not about to happen. Eventually, Darden built across the way on Route 2, and did quite well, but other restaurants have not been so fortunate. The primary reason is that they have fallen to "the last boy on the block syndrome." Often, companies will force feed themselves into markets where all that remain are secondary locations. As an example, just north of our offices in Addison, a town that promoted the development of dinner houses, Darden built three free-standing restaurants, one of which was their fledgling concept China Coast, all after fifty or so restaurants were already on Belt Line Road. Their mistake was made before they were opened. Tucked up against a maddening four way intersection and in plain view of all the traffic, at peak times, it was virtually impossible to get into the site. Restaurants like this died a slow death.

NINE

Up In the Lazy Boys

The four of us were racking up frequent flyer miles on American Airlines at a frantic pace, and apparently our loyalty did not go unnoticed. We all qualified for the new Top Tier program and received Gold Cards along with special first class upgrades in the mail. From this day forward it was up in the Lazy Boys! Yippee! Incidentally, this did signal the end to Tale Wind's services at Gate 62, however, our secret lasted long after his retirement.

Word traveled quickly as Springer called to say that he and Preston had received their Gold Cards and upgrades. They were flying American out to Phoenix on a regular basis looking in on their new shopping center development out on Blue Bell. "Ryan, did you open your mail today?" Springer asked. "Yup, say goodbye to steerage!" I quipped, as he knew that I knew what he was calling about. "Ryan, the boys trip to Vegas next Saturday? You and I know where we'll be sitting." "Yeah, and don't forget Preston; he's coming along isn't he?" "You bet! He can't wait. Can you believe there are 11 of us going?"

The Dallas version of Ocean's Eleven. Springer thought it would be a good way to celebrate his and my November birthdays with a trip to Las Vegas, extending invitations to our friends. The response was overwhelming from the predominantly single crowd that made up our fiefdom. The plan was to fly out on Saturday morning and come back Monday afternoon. The airport rendezvous point was the front door of The Admirals Club. Why not try and slip in with 8 guests? The room would be quiet on a Saturday morning.

Springer, taking on the role of a Boy Scout Troop Leader, turned to the group for a morning debriefing. "Listen up guys, let's go in quietly and the three of us will see if we can't all get bumped up to the front cabin. I can't promise you anything, but why don't you hand over your tickets to me and at the very least we can take care of the boarding passes. Remember, keep the noise down."

The buzzer sounded and Preston led the charge up the stairs to the front desk where we were greeted by two of American's prettiest female employees. "My, my, gentleman, pray tell, where you'all headed this morning?" we were greeted in a wonderful Texas drawl. Her desk mate answered the question for us, saying, "My guess would be these rascals are headed to Las Vegas," as the three of us placed our Gold Cards on the counter.

"We are indeed, is it a light load this morning?" I asked.

"Very," she said.

"You see these fine gentlemen standing behind us?"

"Let me guess - they are all friends of yours?" she replied.

"Indeed!" (Truth be told, there were three or four that Springer was going to introduce me to as soon as we got airborne.) "I know this is a lot to ask," I continued. "Is there any chance that they can ride with us? In the front, I mean."

"Are they going to behave? We are going to hold you three accountable," she said with a grin. Turning back to the group, all it took was a wink of the eye that told them that we were in!

The cabin crew just shook their heads in quiet disbelief as they watched us lay siege to their First Class Cabin. (It makes me think of Sinatra in "Live at the Sands" when he asked his band leader, "How did all these people get into my room?")

The two flight attendants responsible for serving us had to

be thinking on the same lines. "Can we get you anything to drink before we take off? How about a round of Bloody Mary's?" Springer looked back from his bulkhead aisle seat and asked, "Bloody Mary's okay for everybody?" "Yup!" resounded the chorus. Circle the wagons! After breakfast, everyone settled in nicely. The only glitch was that American felt compelled to inform us that the First Class cabin's entire supply of vodka had sorely been depleted and that they were unsure as to how long they could count on the coach cabin as a source of replenishment.

Springer wanted to tend shop for a moment, which was fine by me. A lot of people do business with people they like, and Springer and Preston were two of the good guys. "Ryan, when can we get Viken and Buddy to look at our site in Fort Worth?" they asked.

"Not sure, we've got our hands full with this 20 store schedule," I replied.

"You guys think you can open twenty stores in one year? God Almighty Ryan, can operations handle the load?" they rightfully wondered.

"They seem to think so. It could make or break us. The brand will survive, but we may not!" That subject is for another day.

Springer continued, "Listen, Preston and I have been talking. How about if we send a chopper over to Midway and pick up Viken and Buddy for a tour of The Metroplex? It's the best way to see the market. Looking at aerials doesn't do it justice."

Springer knew I was chasing after Carmine Bushot, owner of Birds Eye View, an aerial photography concern in North Dallas. What he didn't know about was the subtle bomb she dropped in my lap at a recent lunch at The Atlantic Café, coincidentally Springer's favorite Dallas restaurant. "You know something Ryan?" she had asked. "My body wants you, but my mind doesn't." Ouch. At least she was direct; as for me, I was content to have whichever part of her wanted me.

Springer continued selling the helicopter idea. "We should be able to set her down on the vacant lot next door to Midway. It's an Aerospatiale 350. The B3 model seats six comfortably. What do you say?"

"You know something, Buddy and Viken may enjoy going for a ride. Let me talk to Brigid and check his schedule. A Friday afternoon sounds like the best time to do this."

Springer continued, "Just let me know what beverages to bring on board."

"That's easy," I replied. "Sonoma Cutrer Russian River Ranches, and a six pack of Budweiser."

"Consider it done."

Springer had given me an idea. Why not start using choppers in the northeast? That was something to consider.

Most of the guys were taking a vodka induced nap as Springer continued. "Ryan, see that guy sitting behind Touchdown?"

"Yeah," I said. (Touchdown Tommy was a star running back for The Baylor Bears. His career was derailed by a mechanical bull named Jilly who threw him for a loop at a local bar called The Cow Pattie in Waco badly injuring his knee in the process.) "That's Nigel Harrington, our real estate attorney. You watch, as soon as we check in to the DI, he will ask if you want to take a ride out to the Rooster Ranch. You might want to go. They say its a hoot."

"How far a drive is it?" I asked.

"For Nigel, about a six pack!"

"Does Preston know that he goes out there?"

"Of course."

The Desert Inn became one of our favorite places to stay. It had all the trappings of a large casino with a "hometown feel," and as an added bonus, it didn't hurt that Preston was a frequent visitor here during his divorce, and, accordingly, well looked-after by a Pit Boss named Hoard Chips. The Sports Book was far from the largest in town, but you could always find a seat. That was a crucial element for us to consider as Sunday is pretty much an all day and night affair watching the games. Once there, it was every man for himself. It was not like being on cruise ship where dinner is at a certain time, although Springer had made reservations for a large table at the Bum Steer, a relic of a steakhouse off the strip. Springer liked the bar as it was usually infested with middle aged divorcees.

My roommate was Axel Starre. Axel and another furniture rep, Dusty Buchanan, had both made the trip. These guys knew every furniture dealer from Texarkana to El Paso and points in between. A small group of us assembled at a Black Jack table just to get our feet wet. 'Let's pace ourselves.' Axel took up the "third base" position at the table, occupying the seat immediately to the dealer's right. If and when the dealer busted, that was Axel's cue to chime in: "Bye Bye in the Car Car." Can you imagine? Here was a grown man on a Saturday afternoon at a casino far from home coming up with that. Bye Bye in the Car Car!

Springer was right; Nigel was circling the table looking for volunteers for the ride out to the desert. He had Shane Cockman with him. Shane was an Oklahoma boy who married a gal he met at Texas-OU weekend. Preston, who played a lot of golf with Shane, reported that he was hung like a horse. Apparently he became the talk of the locker room over at Ballsonly Golf Club. Buff Leroy, the locker room attendant who is stationed in plain sight of the shower stalls and towel room, was the first to lay eyes on his oversized testes and quickly dispatched a couple of members to take a peak. He knew that certain guys were always looking for an edge, a distraction of sorts to throw another off his game.

One such member was Baby Cats, a leviathan of a man so called for his love of the furry felines, especially strays. Word got out that one day a malnourished cat leaped onto his golf cart and jumped down into the bottom of his beer cooler to lap up much needed water. He promptly named the cat Bogey, reflective of the score he made on the hole, and took him home that afternoon. Bogey lived for 15 years before he was laid to rest at the greenside spot where they met for the first time.

In the locker room that day, Baby Cats walked over to a nearby sink to give it the cursory comb of hair. Heavens to Betsy, Buff wasn't kidding; this guy was carrying around a palm tree with two ripe coconuts. Baby Cats, slapping an energy pill ($20 bill) in Buff's outstretched palm, headed back inside the locker room. "You're not going to believe what I just saw. I mean he was laying each individual ball in the palm of one hand and then talcing with the other." "What do you think we ought to name his unit, Baby Cats? How about Big Luke? "Yeah, that's it. Next time we see him on the first tee, we'll ask him how's Big Luke getting along?"

Was Shane going to the Rooster Ranch to show off his prowess? For me, there was no convincing necessary; it was Bye Bye in the Car Car out to The Rooster Ranch. Now I could understand Nigel's rationale. At least he was getting something in return for his $200. The three of us were on our way.

From my vantage point in the back seat, it was difficult to determine which direction we were headed, but it didn't matter much. The beer was iced down, it was 1 o'clock in the afternoon and we were on our way to The Rooster Ranch. We could forget about the working map for this one day. Nigel was running this show.

"So Ryan, Springer was telling me you work for Friday's. Are you going to look at their site in Fort Worth?"

"Yeah, at some point. We've been busy filling in some holes up in the Northeast. Great market for us up there!"

"Yeah, I've been meaning to take my wife up to Boston or New York. Which city do you prefer?"

"Well, I am partial to Boston because I grew up in South Weymouth, about 13 miles south of the city. Of course, there is nothing like a weekend in The Big Apple.

"So I've heard," he continued. "It will cost me a small fortune as she's not one to walk by too many stores without going inside. Ah, what the hell. Who'd you take in the Tennessee game?"

"The Vols!"

"Okay, then that's who we are rooting for. The Rooster has a TV in the lounge. You can catch the score when we get there!"

"So Nigel, you've been coming out here for awhile?" I asked.

"Oh, sure, long before I was married. Their standards are much higher than before. Hell, be prepared to have your unit examined under a lamp for Christ's sake. You know Shane is looking forward to that." We pulled up. "Je suis arrivee," he said.

An oasis in the desert. Not much more than your typical mobile home, it was strategically positioned on what appeared to be the leeward side of a rocky outcrop. Stepping out of the car here, we got the sense that it could just plain howl out there. "Blow the horns right off a cow," as the Irish tend to say.

The three of us were welcomed as if it was a pleasant surprise. Saturday afternoon, three relatively sober individuals! You could hear the ladies cackling to each other, scrambling to get ready to parade their wares in front of the waiting customers. For me there was no rush, the bar was open, the game was on TV, I could slip some quarters in the juke box.

There were 7 women to choose from as they walked out into the lounge in single file. The two married guys culled two out of the pack and disappeared behind closed doors leaving me with the five remaining prospects. "Care to dance?" I asked. "But of course, I would be delighted," she replied. Here we both were at the Rooster Ranch, cheek to cheek, slow dancing to the Brenda Lee forty-five "All Alone am I." Janice sang the words "All alone am I ever since you said goodbye!" I whispered in her ear "you have such a lovely voice."

"Thanks," she replied, "sang in a gospel choir in New Orleans. My mother, God rest her, got me started when I was little." She paused. "You're different, most guys would be pumpin and dumpin by now. Taking a different tack I see."

"Listen Janice, I'm here to please you," I said.

"Really? Well you know I've been thinking of a word lately," she said. "Oh ya and what word may that be?" I asked.

"I'll give you a hint," she said, as she slowly pirouetted. "The word ends in 'asm.' Come on, my room is the last one on the right," she purred, as she took me by the hand, not waiting for the song to end. The walls were not exactly sound proof, as we slowly crept down the hall. That's when we could hear this exchange; "Well, well, well, Cowboy, you've got yourself some kinda fence post!" Big Luke was under the lamp!

Sadly, I must report that Janice was left on the brink, right on the edge of filling in the blanks __ __ __ from where I was positioned, and from what I could hear [it wasn't gospel music], she had to have gotten as far as 'org.' She wasn't faking it.

The beer was chilled to a perfect temperature by the time we hit the road back to Shangri-La. Shane said, "Dammit Ryan, you were in there a long time."

"Well," I explained, "there was a little foreplay going on out on the dance floor! Did you guys have time to catch the score?"

"Time? We watched the first half." We traveled at high speeds through the barren landscape called the desert. Shane made an attempt at a game: "Pick a number between 1 and 10."

"Five."

"That's not the one I was thinking of, I'll have another beer!"

The essence of the trip was to make it to Sunday in one piece, as that would be the day we would congregate at The Sports Book for NFL Sunday. The purpose of scheduling a Saturday night dinner away from the strip was as the song goes: "Help [us] make it through the night." Although attendance was optional, this was a well attended affair.

Nigel was certain to stay behind as he liked the DI's new Asian Restaurant, Sai Woo. He had talked to a waitress there and learned that the owners were contemplating changing the name as pranksters were calling the restaurant at various hours. When the restaurant would answer the phone "Sai Woo," the prankster would reply, "Woo" and hang up. They suspected hotel guests were getting into the act. The waitress told Nigel that they were instructed to answer the phone with hello, rather than "Sai Woo." Despite that, inevitably, an out-of-the-loop prankster would still call up to say "Woo."

For us the Bum Steer was the place to let our hair down. Owned by Giuseppe Linguini from Binghamton, New York, the decor was what you could call Early Dark. Subdued lighting, deep red upholstered booths, mahogany paneling interrupted on occasion by red velvet wall coverings, ceiling tiles that were painted black to camouflage the nicotine build-up from constant cigar and cigarette smoke, and lest we forget, the nude oil painting that adorned the back bar, a trademark of any worthy saloon.

The DI accommodated us with a shiny new black stretch limousine for the ride. Arriving fashionably late (it's not easy corralling ten guys, a few of which are making last minute bets on the games at the Sports Book), we were greeted into this den of iniquity with open arms. "Mr. P., great to have you back, Springer so lovely to see you. Please have a seat at the bar, your table will be ready shortly. I count ten; is that correct?" "Indeed," said Springer.

An oenophile in his own right, Springer continued on. "Giuseppe, fire up four bottles of our favorite Barolo and start 'em breathing!"

Giuseppe beamed, "We just happened to get a case in last week."

Ten guys filing into the lounge's tight quarters was certainly an eye opener for the regular Saturday night crowd. They had to be wondering if we were conventioneers, though must have known it was unlikely this late in the year. .

Jammed into the corner on an angle was a Baldwin stand-up piano being played by an older gentleman clad in a tuxedo. It made all the difference that he was simply playing the piano and not singing along. Giuseppe didn't want to detract from the dining experience by having obnoxious Tony Bennett wan-a-bees using the lounge as their personal stage.

Giuseppe, with the skill of a border collie, herded us to the boardroom-sized table smack in the middle of the restaurant. It was a situation that made us feel compelled to open our wallets as all eyes were now trained on the ten men ready to gorge on large filets and buckets of full bodied red; there was a false sense of security sitting here as everyone had in the back of their mind that they could be back at The DI headed for the financial abattoir.

Nothing on the menu missed our table. Over-sized shrimp cocktail, jumbo baked potatoes with sour cream and chives, Hearts of Palm salads with Blue Cheese dressing, Oysters Rockefeller by the dozen (gotta keep Big Luke happy), and, of course, New York Strips for ten.

"So did any of you hard dicks jump on Rice University?" Cha ching. Touchdown said, "I knew we should have been all over that bet. Thirty blessed points, come on!" He continued, "How was the Ranch, Jeeeff?

"Spectacular. We all should have gone. Imagine 11 of us showing up on a Saturday afternoon? Tell you what, and I owe Nigel on this one, before I go out on a Saturday night, that's if I can get someone to go out with me, we are gonna jump in the sack and screw our brains out. No really think about it. This way you can be yourself during the evening, and she can do her thing." I thought I was onto something. I continued, "How many times do you find yourself driving home, it's fucking late, one of you or both have had too much to drink, too much to eat or whatever, and then you hear, 'You know Jeff?' 'No, what's that?' 'You made a real asshole out of yourself in front of my friends.' 'Why, what the hell did I do now?' you ask as the effects of the whiskey take hold of your emotions. Now you aren't even thinking about sex. Maybe stopping the car and asking her to get out, but not sex.

Touchdown interjected, "Remember that gal we met at the Wrinkle Room. Shit, I drove her home in her car. She was so drunk, and we got to her driveway and I started fidgeting with the garage door opener, turning it this way and that thinking to myself, Come on open up for Christ sake. Now I've got to ask her how it works. The next words out of her mouth were 'Don't worry, you won't be here long enough.' Fuck, now I'm driving her car. What a nightmare! But I see what you mean. Get it over with in the afternoon."

I continued. "Fellas, I could go on all night about this." "Go ahead," they agreed. "Giuseppe's not going to run out of wine, he said he just got a case in this week."

"This is a great one," I said. "This gal, I think she sold for IBM out in Sandy Lake, she was a tad on the aggressive side. Anyway, she invites me to a house party way out in Coppell for God's sake. She did say in a real classy way, 'Listen, Jeff, you are not going to know anybody here, however, they are all my friends, and you"ll like them. Let me tell ya boys, this gal came out decked to the nines, low cut summer dress, I mean to tell ya, it was Body Heat!" I paused. What was that actress' name? "We get to the party and I give it the old cutesy stuff like "Can I get you another glass of wine."

Dusty observed, "You were cramping her style, Ryan. You should have backed off."

"You're right, Dusty, that is exactly what I was doing." I replied. "She pulls me over to the corner of the room and says, 'Okay, Ryan, listen carefully. I'm going to fuck your brains out when we get home, so relax, got it?' I got it. 'Now, go meet some of my friends.'

"We've got a buddy in the furniture business," Dusty said, "whose mantra is 'Anything we say after 9 o'clock doesn't count.' Think about it, it's brilliant. But I like the afternoon delight business. Now all I have to do his convince my wife. Fuck, it may keep her out of the stores."

"For how long? Ten minutes?" Touchdown asked. "Ryan, tell everybody what that gal said to you when you were prancing around on her water bed."

"Oh you mean Susan? Oh shit. She lives down the street and we had gone out a few times, but then she became a pain in the ass. I get home one night and give her the old "whiskey call." Reluctantly she invites me over. She opens the door and it was right up the stairs, for a belly flop onto the water bed, all giggly and stuff. Laying on my back I'm watching her as she is undressing, She said to me, "Ryan, if I wasn't so drunk and horny, you wouldn't be here right now."

We could hear Preston fire in an order of Bananas Foster for the denouement. That was fine by us, as that would take us past midnight. The room was starting to clear out as we entered the final phase of our dining experience. For a restaurant owner such as Giuseppe, there is a risk-reward in extending the leash on such a rambunctious group dining amongst your Saturday evening regulars. You can be left wondering how many couples occupying your two-tops have gone away disheartened by a tolerant owner. "He doesn't care about us anymore, all he is seeing is dollar signs."

We didn't care; they were our dollar signs and it was our Vegas trip.

Wrapping up the night, Springer signaled for the check, which would be divided 11 ways. After forking over a Honeybee a piece, we would be back in the limo; a cheap date if you look at it the right way. As it turns out, it wasn't going to be quite that simple. Axel and Dusty decided to split the bill in half and pay by credit card. The rest of us would then pay them in cash. This was their effort to bolster their precious cash reserves which were in short supply after an afternoon of gambling and losing. The waiter took the path of least resistance and approached Axel first. "The yellow copy is yours, thank you very much, sir," he said.

Then he headed on over to Dusty, where he whispered something in his left ear. It did not take long for us to realize that there was a little bit of an accounting issue. "What do you mean the card won't go through?" he asked, loudly enough for us all to hear. This took us by surprise as Dusty had a lucrative business representing two or three major high end furniture manufacturers out of High Point, North Carolina. "Run it through again for Pete's sake; I must have a $25,000 line of credit with Citibank!" he told the waiter.

Axel, like the rest of us, couldn't believe what he was hearing. Not one to hold back, he promptly stood up and called the whole dining room to silence, tapping loudly on his glass with his spoon. "Ladies and gentlemen of the Bum Steer—" he began. "Axel, what the hell are you doing?" we whispered. "Ladies and gentlemen," he continued, undaunted, "no good! Did ya hear that? Dusty's credit card is no good! Spent! Done! Emp—"

"Axel, for Christ's sake, sit down!" Springer pulled him down.

The waiter followed Dusty's instructions and ran it through again, but to no avail, and back to the table he came, again with the bad news.

Incensed, Dusty asked to use the phone in Giuseppe's office, adding that he was bringing his attorney with him. "Bernaise Sauce," he said, "You're coming with me. We are calling Citibank, I'll get to get to the bottom of this." Douglas Bernazzi, a.k.a. Bernaise Sauce, a renaissance man in the kitchen, was his lawyer, and was by trade a leasing attorney of all things.

Always thinking of priorities, even in the midst of this embarrassing situation, Dusty continued, "Oh waiter, get us all another round of drinks and start me a new tab." By this time, the table was in hysterics! You can imagine Citibank's reaction to this phone call. Finally, they got to the bottom of it, and the answer didn't disappoint. Doug reported that they had discovered that Dusty's wife went out furniture shopping that afternoon and picked up some fairly large ticket items. Dusty sat down, understandably exasperated by this embarrassing ordeal. "Fellas," he started. "I'm sorry. My Goddamn wife," he said. We nodded. Dusty took a generous sip from his drink, sat back, and gave us one of his favorite lines like only a Dallas guy could: "You know, sometimes I feel like I've been fucked more times than a tied up piece of livestock."

It was getting past our bedtime and had been quite a night. The limo was out front to pick us up. After a quick check of the hockey score with the bartender, we thanked Giuseppe, and told him we'd see him back there next year. Arrivederci for now, Bum Steer!

"Death is nature's way of telling you to slow down." We may have benefited from listening to that advice, but Sunday morning we awoke very much alive, so it was off to the Sports Book for, optimistically, a full day of betting.

"Have the French Toast because that may be the only chance to dine for the rest of the day," Axel joked over a cup of coffee.

Shane had just joined us. "Boys, wouldn't it be just great to get off to a good start today?" Touchdown Tommy threw a little early morning jab in Dusty's direction. "Better hurry up and pay for that breakfast with that other credit card of yours; the stores are about to open in Dallas!"

No surprise, Nigel, a late arrival downstairs, looked the most rested. Shane asked, "So, did you go back for seconds?" "No," he said, "but I did at Sai Woo. Fabulous restaurant."

"So fellas," he continued. "How was The Bum Steer? Any good stories?"

"Ask Doug," I said. "I believe he will be invoicing Dusty when he gets back to the office."

Next, all eleven were present and accounted for at The D.I. Sports Book. No seat assignments, we just plunked ourselves down, like we owned the seats. Preston made the first good call of the day: Greyhounds! Not the dogs, the drinks. He figured it wouldn't fill us up as fast, just vodka and grapefruit juice, after all. Perfect.

Shane chimed in, "Isn't that a Salty Dog?" to which Preston replied, "Not unless you put salt around the rim, Dumbass." I'm not sure when and where we first heard that pseudonym; however, we had a lot of fun with it. Put into context, for us, it was truly a sign of affection towards the other person. Unlike American Airlines, The DI wasn't about to run out of vodka. If it was Stolichnaya and Grapefruit that you wanted, then there was a pretty good chance that you would be dreaming in Russian sometime within the next few hours.

The East Coast games were just about ready to kick off. Axel, a Pittsburgh native, liked the Steelers at home over their archrival Cincinnati Bengals. The game was about to be played in a blinding snowstorm, so the consensus was that this would be a low scoring game. Our money was on the Under, in this case, if the total combined points scored for both teams was less than 35, we would win. It didn't matter who won the game; we just didn't want anyone to score a lot of points.

That wasn't the opinion of an "outsider" sitting in front of us. On the very first play of the game, Steelers full back Franco

Harris was running a sweep around the right end when this guy yelled out "Get out of bounds." Come on, we thought, this is the first play of the game. Well, he bet the right way and we didn't. The final score was 35-14 Steelers. Another round of Greyhounds!

Maybe we should have gone out the back door of the DI, as the unthinkable was about to happen. My roommate, Axel, was about to lose 11 bets in a row. O for Nada! Trying to keep a humorous spin on his misfortune, Axel held up his watch and said, "Could be worse. If I was home right now, I would be heading over to The Phone Company Lady's house, that miserable ...!" Axel, like me, a lifelong bachelor, always thought that marriage was an overrated pastime. My old golfing buddy and divorce lawyer friend Whisperin' Will said it best when he said to his friend and client (from his first marriage) while on the way out the door with him to his second wedding, "Jack, how did you feel this morning when you took your last shit with the door open?"

That night, Dallas was playing at Kansas City. We just had to hang around for that one. By now we were all VIP'S at the DI. Hoard stopped by to visit with us, mainly to inquire about dinner plans. It was obvious by the group's reaction that nobody wanted to give up our front row seats. So we decided to call Domino's. Sausage and Pepperoni was agreed upon. Goes to show that Las Vegas is a city of firsts; in our case, we called the first pizza delivery to The Sports Book, at least for us anyway.

A smattering of KC fans standing in the way back were performing that occasional Indian ritual (Na na na na na na na!), all with the chopping motion. We were hearing it too many times as Dallas was struggling to cover the 6 point line. Dallas quarterback Danny White, in a desperate attempt to lead the team back in the last two minutes, threw an interception on the KC 15 yard line. As the corner back was scampering down the sideline looking like Bob Hayes of old, Preston, in a voice of desperation, yelled, "Somebody better get him!" But, nobody got him.

Axel, appearing very pale, said to me, "Ryan, call American; let's blow this pop stand tonight!" There couldn't be anybody on the red-eye on a Sunday evening, I thought, as I fumbled for the phone. I delivered the news to Axel: "The good news is that we have reservations, the bad news is that they can't take care of our seating arrangement until we get to the gate."

"Let's get out of here," he eagerly said. "I'd much rather sit in an airport bar than this hell hole." He was really looking pale. "Goddammit, Ryan, 11 in a fucking row!"

Just as we were about to leave the room, the phone rang. "Ryan, it's me, Springer. I'm coming with you guys! See you downstairs." Click! I told Axel that Springer would be joining us. A friend of Springer since their S.M.U. days, Axel guessed the poor bastard had just lost it all in Black Jack. We found each other downstairs, and the three of us piled into a cab and headed for McCarran. Turning the corner for the homestretch to our gate, it was clear that we were not the only losers leaving town. We were about to participate in a Las Vegas version of the Exodus.

I took charge. "Okay, boys, hand me your tickets, and I'll look into the seating arrangements." Axel, by now having taken on the persona of an unhealthy looking Ratso Rizzo in Midnight Cowboy, pointed to a sign over the bar across from the gate. "Lookie here! Glenlivet Special, 3 for 1. Boys, perhaps our luck is a changing!" Perked up, he told me, "Ryan good luck, we'll order for ya!"

Saying a quick prayer that the agent might half resemble Tale Wind, I approached the counter. "Hi there, what are they giving away tonight?" I asked, as I presented our tickets along with the two gold cards to a spectacular looking gate agent. "I do not know Mr. Ryan, all of a sudden it just got crazy," she replied. "How was your stay?"

"Well, my compadres are about to drown themselves in

scotch across the hall, if that tells you anything," I joked.

"Be careful," she warned. "We don't want to have to carry you guys on the plane!" She handed me the boarding passes. "Come back and see us," she said. Was that a wink? No time to lose; I headed to the bar.

Springer greeted me with a plea: "Tell me we are sitting in the Lazy Boys," as I handed him over the tickets. "It's too unbearable for me to look," I replied.

He looked, and sure as hell, we were up in the Lazy Boys. "Sit down and relax, Ryan, you're like a fish out of water," he said. Just at that moment a tray of nine Glenlivets arrived at our table. Happy Trails, as we toasted the first round. Three three-for-one specials later, we got up to leave the bar and traverse the airport floor to our gate. The waiter, having just served us the special, perhaps more quickly than he was accustomed to serving this special, watched us get up to leave, and saw Axel stumble a bit. "Have a nice flight," he said, paused, and continued, "...to the gate!" We got quite a kick out of that.

Springer and Axel were acting somewhat sedated as we boarded the DC-10, but I had a major Glenny induced cackle going and it was loud. Passed down from my mother and her mother before her, we could really stretch the cords. I recall a similar situation where the cackles took hold of me at Dangerfield's club in Manhattan. Standing at the bar next to Baby Cats, a comedian had me going in a fit of laughter at which time Rodney walked by and said, "Cheer up, will you, boys."

Axel slipped into the window seat next to me, Springer the aisle seat behind us. An older fellow, sitting by the window in front of Axel, stuck his head above the seat just enough where you could see it, and registered a noise complaint directly at Axel. "Listen, I am old, tired and sick," he said, "and I do not enjoy hearing all this commotion." Axel replied, "Well if you're that sick, I suggest you get off the plane and check yourself into a hospital." End of story. Not our most respectful moment, but didn't this man know that laughter is the best medicine?

American quickly dimmed the cabin lights once we reached our assigned altitude and it was nighty night for most of us. Axel must have awoken first as I noticed that he had left his seat. He was gone for the longest time, prompting me to ask Springer if he had seen or heard from him. Springer, in laconic fashion, certainly a trademark of his, replied, "Nope, probably back in coach." Glancing up we could see the sign indicating "lavatory occupied." Just when I happened to look, the door opened and out he came. It was dark, but something was noticeably different about him as he worked his way past me to his seat. He had his customary white shirt on, that I could see. Axel favored the white 100% cotton dress shirt from Ralph Lauren; he thought it handled the Texas heat the best. But why are his sleeves rolled up? I wondered. I asked him if he was okay.

"I am now!" he replied.

"What happened to you?" I asked.

"You are not going to believe this," he shot back. "Come on, tell me," I urged, as I tried to pry whatever ailed him out of his system.

Now, sheepishly, he continued, "Well, after being over served the nine Glenlivets I had to relieve myself. So as I stood there to piss, I must have passed out. With no where to fall in such cramped quarters, I simply slid down the door. When I woke up, I noticed a brown streak running from the crotch of my Docker khakis all the way down to my Ostrich boots. It was quite apparent that I had pissed all over myself. Now standing up, a little hung over mind you, I yanked my money clip and car keys out of my pockets just to make sure I still had everything. The next thing I hear it 'CLANG!' Fuck—there go my keys into the toilet. Shit, my whole life is on that chain—Mom's keys, the keys to the Jag, even the bitch's keys. (Axel's reference to The

Phone Company Lady). I rolled up my shirt sleeves, genuflected and reached in after them. Swishing around—hell—I must have tried at least five times. So now you know why the blue arm."

"Well, maybe American can somehow extract them from the tank when we land," I suggested.

And now the shock. "No bother, I got 'em myself!"

"Springer, you've got to hear this!"

After telling Springer the details, I began once again drifting off to sleep, as my mind kept replaying the events of the weekend to the sounds of the theme song from Ocean's Eleven sung magnificently by Sammy Davis Jr. E Oh E-Eleven eleven eeehleven. By the morning, images of the Rooster Ranch would be replaced by colorful copies of the working map, and the sounds of Sammy Davis Jr. would be muted by the hum of the phones.

TEN

Whirlybird

"Jeff, Ben Springer is holding on the other line, and it sounds like it's urgent. Something about a helicopter ride!"

Betty's phone voice wasn't exactly what you would call sexy. If anything, it leaned more toward the Edith Bunker end of the spectrum. If an award were to be given out for Sexiest Phone Voice of the Year, it would have to go to a Retail Leasing Specialist in California named Veronica. A real estate broker friend of ours kept tabs on this unusual category and called to give us a report, "Guys call this number, un-fucking-believable. If you don't want to speak with her, just hang up the phone," he said. "Oh that's nice, just hang up; where's your phone etiquette?" I shot back. "Thanks for the tip, maybe later." Without a doubt, I kept her number right in front of my phone.

"Springer, how are ya!" I said as I picked up the line.

"Have you spoken to Tidy Bowl?" he asked.

"Who?"

"That's my new name for Axel," he said. "We will have to see if it sticks." We laughed, recalling his dirty adventure in the airplane bathroom. "Oh, here's another one for the books," he said. "When I went outside the other morning to get the newspaper, I found it sitting atop my luggage in the driveway. Must have paid the cab and then just left it there. You know, I thought I heard someone honking a horn. Anyway, just shows you what a safe town Carrollton is." Now onto business. "Are we confirmed for Friday?"

"Yes, Sherwin is going to stay behind," I said. "Our new CFO wants to go with us. His name is Ledger Cockbill, nice guy, you'll like him. Bring an extra wine glass! Oh and Springer, you've got to hear this gal's phone voice. She lives in California. Write down this number. See you on Friday."

Blaze was sitting attentively at his desk and got the gist of the conversation. "Fabulous work on the chopper ride, now let's see if we can make this happen where it counts."

Blaze was right. The Texas Tour-Dallas and Houston-was fine and dandy, but there were critical site approvals in New Jersey, Connecticut, on Long Island, and in Massachusetts that took precedent. So often the Ukraine is called Russia's bread basket; the Northeast was the breadbasket for Friday's. We both agreed that a chopper ride over Huntington, Long Island was overkill. "You know, Blaze," I said, "I'm glad we don't necessarily need one here because I wouldn't have the balls to ask that attorney. The deal is teetering as it is. Can you hear his response? 'Sure, right away, Jeff, in fact from my office window, I can see the helipad on top of The Met Life Building. Wave to me when you get there; we'll send over Mayor Koch's private chopper to take us all to the fucking potato fields of Suff-uck County.'

"They discontinued chopper service from that building in 1977 for Pete's sake," Blaze recalled. "Don't you remember the accident? Not sure if they were landing or taking off, but it had to have been too windy. Shit, one of the blades may have embedded in the side of the building. It was a mess."

"Needn't worry. Sherwin will see his way through this one no sweat. Albany, Warwick, we'll be three for three here pretty soon."

"Come on, Ryan," he replied. "Let's not get ahead of ourselves. The terrain in the northeast is such that it would be difficult for Sherwin, Buddy or most anybody that has not spent a great deal of time there to understand our decision making."

Blaze was right. Clearly we would have to retrace all our steps, and then some, and that's where the whirlybird came in handy. The drill was to bring along the working map and let the chopper do the work. Developers were receptive to picking up the tab for these charters, short money when you consider the long term ramifications, not to mention the fact that they were already prepared to fork over one million dollars to make a deal happen. If a chopper ride gives us a better shot, then let her rip.

We caught a classic fall day for this eventful trip. Temperatures in the low 80s clear skies, atypical for Dallas. The sound of the Aerospatiale approaching Midway caused quite a stir both inside and outside of the office. We could tell Viken and Buddy were getting a charge out of this. Watching this sleek piece of machinery descend on our HQ made the people in the office even more proud to be are a part of something special.

Springer, our gracious host, provisioned the whirlybird to a tee. If you have ever traveled with restauranteurs, then you know about the constant desire to eat. You want to see grumpy? Try depriving one of these guys of food for an extended period of time.

The first leg of our trip was west over the L.B.J. Freeway towards Fort Worth where we would fly over the 20,000-acre former Carpenter Ranch. A modest sized spread in the process of being developed into a master planned community called Las Colinas (Spanish for "the hills"). A project that required a vision beyond most people's comprehension. The infrastructure alone was mind boggling. Texans think big and this was Big with a capital B. First came the road network as at the beginning there were none to speak of, followed by man-made lakes interspersed with canals with docking facilities for boat traffic. Buddy observed, "Looks like they are preparing an anchorage for The Godstad," jokingly making reference to Viken's yacht. Now add championship golf, equestrian and bike trails and you've got yourself a world-class live and work environment.

The single most important generator of revenue for Friday's? Rooftops, dwellings. Las Colinas had this in many forms, from luxury garden apartments to multi-million dollar estates. It was the classic 'let's all work and play all behind the same fence' syndrome. No need to rush in the morning to catch your Braniff flight to Caracas. The dual runways of D.F.W. were a drivable par five away. Spitting distance, to use Texas parlance.

Viken spoke first. "Springer, the office tower by the lake with the herd of Mustangs..." Life sized bronze statues of galloping mustangs fording an imitation stream were placed at the foot of the tallest building, and soon became the signature icon of the development. Viken continued, "Are there tenants moving in or is it a 'see thru?'"

Springer responded, "It's going to be a while before that dog hunts referring to the building's occupancy. But eventually it will hunt." Texans use a great deal of hunting dog analogies in their everyday conversation. Springer and the boys favored shooting birds to anything else, quail mostly. It required the skill of highly trained bird dogs to be successful, and they loved their dogs. "What do you think, Ryan?"

"Buddy," I said. "We should definitely be here. Look at all the residential under construction, then add offices, hotels, and shopping to the mix."

"These folks have called us several times," I said, "and I've been out to visit with them. Granted it is a little green right now but it's going to fill in. Just look at the airline personnel alone that live here. I used to date a gal that flies for British Caledonia. She lives down there."

Springer remembered. "Joanie was her name. You brought her to my pool party remember? Goddamn, Ryan, she was a doll. Why did you burn that bridge?" Some guys leave a span of hope—not me. If you're going to blow the bridge, then blow the bridge.

"Let's not go there, I said. "If I think about it, I just may end it right here and now. Probably land right on that mustang."

Viken piped up. "Ever been married, Ryan?"

Oh, here we go, I thought. "No," I said.

"Why not? Afraid of committment?"

"Probably," I said.

Viken, probing a weakness, persisted. "What do you mean probably? You are afraid to commit."

When would this line of questioning end, I wondered. Just then, Buddy asked, "You see that vacant lot right in the center of the development. What are they going to put there?" he asked. Phew, subject changed.

"Buddy," I said, "that is where they envision their first major restaurant tenant and, from my experience of driving the market, that is the eye of the hurricane, the 100%! They even had the foresight to build an air conditioned tunnel under the street that connects the office tower to the restaurant. It's their version of the skywalk system that you see in Minneapolis, except that instead of avoiding the cold you can avoid the heat."

"So what's holding us back here, Ryan?" he asked as Springer signaled the pilot to head west to H.E.B. (Hurst, Euless, and Bedford). The meter was running and we hadn't been to his project. Springer knew that he would have to expend some goodwill before he could pounce on his objective, the site in Fort Worth. He wasn't about to panic.

In response to Viken's question, I began, "Well a couple of things might be holding us back. As is typical in these types of projects, parking is an afterthought. No offense Springer, but sometimes developers suffer from megalomania."

"Wait a minute where did you go to school?" Ledger asked, "using such big words and all." Ledger was enjoying this payback. "Northeastern University in Boston, for only two and half years!" I said. Ledger reflected. "Okay, that makes more sense. So we hired you because you know the streets of Boston and not so much for the big words. Springer, how about you? Have you lived here all your life?"

"Not yet," he said. "No, actually born and raised in Dallas, went to S.M.U."

Ledger asked, "Does that really stand for Suck Me Unconscious?" We laughed. "Ever been married, Springer?"

"Once, no kids."

"You know," Ledger said, "I'd liked to be married someday. When did you know it wasn't going to work?"

Springer thought about it. "When I saw her walking down the aisle."

"You mean the church aisle?" asked Ledger, incredulously. "I do I mean the church," he replied. Ledger wanted to learn more, as did Viken and Buddy."

"Let me picture this," said Ledger. "You are standing at the altar with your best man by your side. The music starts and she starts heading down the aisle." At that moment, Buddy interrupted by singing "Here she comes just a walking down the street-singing do a diddy diddy dum diddy do-I'm so happy and that's how it's going to be-singing do a diddy diddy dum diddy do- she looks fine- looks fine..."

Ledger continued his cross examination. "Did you think about bailing out?"

"It may have crossed my mind," he said, as Buddy continued the song "and then it really crossed by mind." Springer, now making light of the situation, asked what the next words were. Before long, we were all singing, pilot included, having a grand time.

To answer your question, Springer said, "Today, for sure, I would have pulled the rip cord. Anyway Ledger, there are plenty of fish in that pond down below!"

Buddy changed the subject to football, saying, "The football team is ranked #4 isn't it?"

"Yeah," Springer replied, "that may change. We've got Notre Dame on the schedule. The trap may be set. Ryan, you coming with us to South Bend?"

"Maybe," I said, trying to refocus. "As I was saying guys, for the parking, you would have to rely on valet. Buddy, what do you think about valet?"

"I don't know; that's a tough one, probably not for us. Ryan, get back to us on this."

"Roger that. Springer, where we headed?"

"West to HEB. We'll fly over the communities of Hurst, Euless, and Bedford and then swing around north to northeast and then back to Midway."

Unlike Dallas where the predominant growth was heading to the north, it would take a while for North Fort Worth to catch up since for years the prevailing wind from the south carried the unpleasant work of The Stockyards in that direction. The bottom line was that from our vantage point in the air, both Dallas and Fort Worth were growing and this was a great way to keep tabs on it. Viken and Springer sat across from each other and were busy discussing wines. Viken can seem aloof unless you push the right buttons. Ledger Cockbill, our newly appointed C.F.O. and young whippersnapper from Hermosa Beach, California, seized the opportunity in close quarters to become more acquainted. Financial analysis is a critical component of our world and as the company's #1 numbers cruncher, his input in that area was welcomed.

Ledger started off poorly with me but finished strong. "So, Jeff, have you heard of Regression Analysis? Some companies are using it as part of their site selection criteria."

Trying to remain as polite as possible my response was terse. "I have, people that do not know what they are doing use it all the time. Seriously Ledger, we cannot make our Real Estate decisions based upon some computer that is fed a bunch of crap and then spits out more crap. Nothing can replace our work on the ground, nothing ever will. Let me put this to you another way. My visits to the west coast of Ireland take me to an enchanting seaside village called Waterville, located on the famed Ring of Kerry. It is known for its world class links, however, the fishing isn't too shabby either. Over several pints at The Butler Arms Hotel bar, I asked a local fishing guide, 'How does a salmon know how to find its way from feeding in waters as far away as Iceland back here to Waterville?' Looking right into my eyes, he answered my question with one word. 'Instinct.' Ledger, it is difficult to tell an analyst at Oppenheimer that our Real Estate is based on gut feelings. Nobody has the balls to say that—I know. This is why restaurant companies are pissing away thousands and thousands of dollars on shit like this, trying to impress the analysts." Fortunately no one took an interest in Ledger's overture and he quickly changed the subject. I meant what I said and left it at that. Yes, you look at demographics and, yes, you look at the key components of those demographics [for us it was per capita incomes], but only as a backup to the homework you have done on the ground.

Viken reported that he was getting a "beaver shot" from a swimming pool raft. Springer asked the pilot to circle for a closer look. Helicopter pilots call it "slapping air" the noise the blades make when the chopper turns on an angle, something about losing "air resistance." This gal knew she had been spotted from above, but, undeterred, she reacted as if saying to us, "I've been expecting you boys."

Buddy said, "Come on wave, yeah there it is, she's waving at us!" her other arm acting as a rudder to lend the pilot an assist. Viken spotted the bathing suit next to the pool.

Now with a glass of wine, Ledger shook off the minor blow

he took earlier and reentered the fray, a mark of a solid guy. He asked Springer, "how much are those houses going for down below?"

"With or without the girl on the raft?" we laughed.

"$250,000."

"Shit," he said, "that's pond scum compared to Hermosa Beach." Pond scum? New word for me, I thought. He just may fit in!

Buddy, leaning towards me and enjoying every moment of this, said in a low voice, "We'd like to tour New Jersey with you in one of these. Can we do it in a half a day?"

"Of course!" I said.

"Make it happen!" he replied. "And another thing, Ryan. See if you can find a developer who can fly our D.V.P for the Southwest, Shoe Wagner, around Houston especially up by Greenspoint. We may have screwed up by building in the middle of two markets. You'd do well to get old Shoe in one of these. He'll tell you right up front he doesn't like to fly. "We know just who to call." He looked out the window. "Springer, is that your shopping center development under construction?" It was. "Can we set her down?" Buddy asked the pilot. Ledger chimed in, "Doesn't look like a good idea; they're pouring what is that, Springer, concrete?"

"That's ok, we'll throw up a little bit of dust, won't harm anybody."

Buddy added, "Reminds me of a joke, but we can wait until we head back."

"No, no let's hear it for Christ sake." Viken loved new material and used it frequently.

As the chopper was setting down Buddy continued, "Travis and Bowie climbed up on the parapet of the Alamo one sunny morning only to overlook the expanse and discover that several thousand Mexicans had assembled off in the distance.

With coffee in hand, Bowie turned to Colonel Travis and said 'I didn't know we were pouring concrete today.'"

We stepped from the chopper into a venerable dust bowl. Construction crews were running for cover. BumBumBumBumBum. Landing like a butterfly with sore feet we gave Springer his due. This was his show and he performed admirably. As Jack Webb used to say in Dragnet "just the facts" and that was all we were asking for.

We continued on to the far reaches of North Dallas, then back south along the old railroad bed that is now The North Dallas Toll Road right above Ballsonly Golf Club. Viken, an accomplished blue water sailor and non-golfer, asked, "No women allowed, I heard?" Springer replied, "Indeed. I think Valentine's Day may be the only day that they are permitted on the grounds, or is it Christmas Eve? I'll find out. You know, they used to host The Byron Nelson Golf Classic. Goddamn, Ryan, remember the Southwest Airlines stews used to serve drinks in the tent." How could I not? "We asked one of them once, 'What time does the band start?' and she replied, 'As soon as the last putt drops.' Guys," he continued. "you'd like this one. Ryan's in the nineteenth hole with us and one of the founding members asks him 'Where you from anyway, Jeeeff," in a very distinct Texas drawl. 'Boston, sir,' Jeff replies. 'Boys, we are guarding the wrong river!' he says."

We were back at HQ. The chopper pilot bid us goodbye and flew south in the direction of Love Field. Springer and I kibitzed in the parking lot. "Ryan, that was fun. All great guys by the way. Listen, as soon as you get your arms around the northeast, we may be able to revisit Fort Worth. We know you have your hands full at the moment. Things are moving so fast. Anyway, just give us the heads up when you're ready. You know we can deliver."

"Oh there's no question about that," I said.

"How's the hunting up there? Are they happy with what you're doing? It's got to be a whole different ball game finding locations in that neck of the woods.

"It certainly is," I said. "Not everything is in front of you like it is here. Although, I'll tell you Springer, the beauty of operating up there is once we take hold, we're like a moray eel, we are not going to let go. The other guys are sure to follow the scent; we've already done their homework for them. We say good luck trying to find a location that is not already secondary to ours."

"Who else is up there from here, Ryan?"

"Steak and Ale has done a decent job in New Jersey, but the concept is tiring."

"Fuck, why don't they put windows in the joint; it just may freshen the concept," said Springer in frustrating tones. "They should start right here with the one next to you guys on Belt Line. Hell, Axel takes the Phone Company Lady in there, only when she stops putting out mind you, because no one he knows goes in the place! Oh and Bennigan's real estate guys have been nosing around, but they aren't impressing anyone that we can see. Poor bastards, it doesn't take long for developers to realize that they would rather have the Real McCoy instead of the imitation. In fact, Blaze and I drove by a Bennigan's site on the North Shore of Boston that they built on a strip of land between a major highway. Peabody, Massachusetts, that's the town. Springer, you could pull out of their parking lot with that black Fleetwood of yours and get spun around like a top, all in broad day light. The same goes for pulling into the place. Can you imagine after a few cocktails, and when it's dark! Say goodbye to two million when you consider the site work that was involved. Chili's, on the other hand is sitting on the sidelines. For how long we aren't sure. Have you met John Titus, their Director of Real Estate?"

"Of course, great guy." he said.

"So I've heard," I said.

"Ryan, he has another guy that works for him that travels

up your way. He is probably on the same flight and you don't even know it."

"Oh, you mean Marvin Braddock. How about we meet him for cocktails one night?" "I'll set it up," he said. "Anyway, Viken thinks that Chili's is struggling with the cost of the liquor license in New Jersey."

"How much are they?"

"You recall me talking to Buddy about a chopper trip in New Jersey? Thanks to you by the way he's agreed to go for it. Well the site in Princeton for example may end up costing us $400,000 for the license. And the other site in Watchung $175,000, give or take. That's assuming that we can locate a willing seller. Ledger by the way, did you hear the fucking part about Regression Analysis? Well anyway, he came up with the idea of carrying them on the books as an asset. You have to give him credit on that one. As for Dallas and Houston, well with the "ease of entry" and all, the chances are out there to stub your toe. Interstesting stuff! You know what they always say 'Just win baby.' Listen," Springer said. "I am meeting Tidy Bowl down at that new wine bar St. Martin's on Lower Greenville. Come join us. Let me see if anybody else is around. Claus's car is still here. You know he just leased an apartment over near there on one of the M streets?"

"Oh, is he out of that big house on Drexler already?"

"Yeah, he was halved last week," he said, referring to Claus's divorce.

"A good looking guy like Claus won't have any problem, especially in Big D. Tell him to get back in town for Thursday nights. That is The Night in Dallas. It's like shooting fish in a barrel! When you see him tonight ask him about The Snake Lady."

The normal route to the Real Estate Department was to take the immediate left past reception and walk down the hall on the left hand side—this was know as "Running The Gaunlet" Buddy's office then Viken's and the corner office of Dalton Scruggs eerily kept vacant since his departure for no reason other than no one was big enough to fill his shoes, I imagine. The western style furnishings and Belgian area rug were all there, the only thing missing was a body. Three more offices and a Conference Room and you were at Betty's desk. Human Resources was one of the three. Bewly thought the office should have one of those seedy motel "Vacancy" signs above the door on a perpendicular angle to the hallway.

The cowardly move is to take the circuitous route, navigating your way by the modesty paneled offices of Purchasing and Accounting, but you couldn't accomplish this without a good old fashion ribbing from Bob Grinder, Director of Purchasing. An office mole of sorts, nothing got by him. He was there six days a week and sometimes on Sundays. The only thing that Friday's bought locally was dairy products, and other than that, Grinder was Sgt. Crapgame's counterpart in Kelly's Heroes. He procured everything. Inundated with product samples of every kind imaginable, the inside of his office looked like a Food Bank. Salesmen desperate to get their feet in the door would park in front, leave the car running, open the trunk and drop a product off at reception. "Bob Grinder asked me to drop this off, would you kindly see that he gets it?" someone would say. The receptionist knows that they have never met, but, not wanting to offend would reply, "Of course, thanks for thinking of Friday's, enjoy your day."

Grinder was a master of the verbal jab. "What's the matter Ryan, afraid that they might see you?" he'd say. "Fuck you are getting to be like Sherwin and Claus, coming this way all the time now. How's Claus doing by the way? We do not see much activity in California on the development schedule? Getting too much sun is he?"

"Leave him be, he's going through a divorce besides he's got a tought assignment," I said.

Grinder suffered from halitosis. You want to keep a safe

distance. If you have fed your dog Cod Liver Oil (to shine their coat) you have experienced this fish smell on their breath. Grinder's breath was similar in nature. They say the polite thing to do is leave a bottle of Listerine on a person's desk when they are not around. Bob was about to get another product to sample. Turning around to go back the other way, "See you pal, come on over and visit sometime!"

Everyone was standing outside Viken's office. Buddy led off, "Nice trip, Ryan. Unusual helicopter. What, no Bell Jet Ranger, they build em right here in Fort Worth!" Viken added, "Aerospatiale, neat bird. Okay, Ryan," he continued. "Las Colinas?"

I answered, "Fellas, we would knock the cover off the ball, but eventually the parking would become a deterrent and with the amount of development going on out there, it wouldn't take long before we were at risk."

Ledger, not missing his chance, said, "Some day you'll have to fill us in on British Caledonia!"

"Attend one of my therapy sessions and you can learn all about her," I said. That should get him thinking as I made my way past! "Hey Claus, where are the rest of the boys?"

Claus answered, "Blaze took the wife back to Erie for the weekend and Bewly—who knows."

"Come down to St. Martin's with us," I said.

"Shit Ryan, that's a wine bar. Do they even serve Dewars?"

"We'll find ya one! It will do you good."

"What about Sherwin?"

"He's back playing tennis. Must be thinking of his days at Texas Tech. Hope he doesn't try and jump over the net. Shit, he couldn't jump over the Sunday newspaper," Claus joked. "You know I just leased a condo over on McComb, I can walk home from that joint."

St. Martin's was not designed to be a singles bar. It was a mid-priced restaurant featuring a sophisticated menu and wines from all over the world. We spent our share of late Friday afternoons here before working our way back to North Dallas. Claus, Axel, Springer, and I kicked back at one of several round tables.

"So Claus, Ryan tells me all four of you guys parachuted into San Francisco."

A dejected Claus, still sporting from the move out of the mini mansion, replied, "Yeah we did, damn near killed myself over the bridge."

"Where were you, Tiburon?"

"I wish. No we were further north in Mill Valley. Goddamn Bewly got me in trouble. This gal was just trying to do a good deed by helping jump start my car and the next thing I know her engine is practically on fire, or it least it seemed that way. Her car engine looked like one of our Shermans after taking a round from a Tiger Tank. It was messy."

Axel, who drove 30,000 miles a year, sensed what went wrong. "Let me guess, you had the negative on the positive and all that?" Claus nodded, "Must have, sparks were flying in every direction like fireflies. Ryan and Blaze raced across the bridge to come to my rescue. Could have been *A Bridge Too Far*, any of you guys ever read it? Cornelius Ryan wrote it just before he died." Claus liked to talk history, as did we. It was escapism. "How about *The Longest Day*? He wrote that too."

Meanwhile Axel noticed a table of three ladies eavesdropping on our conversation. "Boys," he proclaimed, "don't look now, but we have made contact." He'd wait for the proper opening. Claus continued, "It was Rommel's comment about the ensuing invasion that gave him the idea for the book's title. Something about if the first twenty-four hours didn't go well for Germany, he told his aid it would be the longest day."

Axel's resistance broke down. "What kind of wine do we have going over there ladies?"

"Oh," the gal closest to Axel replied. "Just a little friendly

Clos Du Bois.

Springer added, "That's French for Close the Door."

"Very clever. Look girls, we are sitting next to a table of bilingual history buffs."

Claus, unsure of his attitude towards the opposite sex, managed to play along, at first anyway.

"That blonde has a mane on her that won't quit. See that, Ryan," he said.

"I do, she had to have just come from the hairdresser," I said. "Ask her."

"No, now is not the right time. Let them enjoy the wine," he said.

"Well at least they have the sense to drink red wine," I said. "Shit, half these cuckoo clocks think that because they are female they have to drink white wine. They do not realize that it fucks them all up."

Axel added, "You know you are onto something Ryan. The Phone Company Lady and I are at Steak and Ale last Sunday night and she started bawling her brains out, right in the middle of dinner. After two glasses of Gallo she dragged me aboard the emotional roller coaster. We went for a ride that would put the Shock Wave at Six Flags to shame."

Claus asked "How long have you been going out with her? Better still, what's the attraction?"

"Eight years, but we really don't go out. We'll go to the Steak and Ale maybe four times a year if that's what you call going out. No, we have this once a week routine. Every Sunday night after 60 minutes, I get in my car, drive to her house and we fuck, then I come home. The truth be known, my only attraction to her is her tits."

Claus was flabbergasted. "God Almighty sakes, I've got to find me a situation like that! We all do!"

"Claus, I heard you've been halved. How'd that come about?"

Claus launched into a story. "Well, I guess I should have seen it coming. One night, I came home really late—I mean very late—I thought I'd be safe since my wife goes to bed early. Not so. I tiptoe into the house only to find her in the living room."

"Well, what did you say?" Axel asked.

I said, "Harriet, in lieu of a prepared speech, I will now accept questions from the floor."

We all laughed. Claus was back on the wine discussion. "Ryan, so what you are saying is steer the gals toward reds not whites."

"Exactly, all I know," I said, "is that every glass of white wants to be a red! Don't get me wrong, you can start out with a nice glass of white and then jump across the stream, but any time you're with a gal that starts firing too many white wines down the hatch, either place a large goblet of robust red in front of her, or run for the truck."

Axel jumped in, "What was that W.C.Fields line? 'I once met a woman who drove me down the road to drink. I forgot to write and thank her for it.'" Goddamn that's a great one. Axel looked over at the girls next door, who incidentally were on their second bottle of wine. "Are you gals listening to our conversation?"

"Oh you mean something about W.C.Fields?"

"Yup, they're listening."

Claus said to me, "Ryan, the blond is wearing red pumps. You know what that means."

I said nothing.

"Damn, Ryan, she reminds me of that gal from The Crescent?"

"Why did you have to remind me?"

Claus continued, addressing the table now, "Ryan and I decide to head down the Toll Road to The Crescent on a Thursday night. Anyway, Ryan bird dogs this gal—"

Axel interrupted, saying to me, "By the way, nobody bird dogs like you can. If only you could close."

Springer piped up, "From now on, we are calling him Fetch! That may stick!"

Claus, "Go ahead Ryan, you tell 'em the story."

I picked up where he left off. "This gal was wearing red pumps, just like this gal next door. It's a school night and all, so we have to get going. Claus leaves, but not before asking if I needed a ride. Twice he asked me—I might add—and he was declined twice. Now, Miss Red Pumps was going to take me home, or at least that was the plan anyway. She had the new Beamer heading out of the parking lot and yours truly as a passenger. I proceeded to tell her that I lived in Carrollton and that it would probably be easier to jump on the Toll Road. She asked if I minded stopping for cigarettes first. 'Of course not.' She pulls into the parking lot of this bar called Balboa's and says 'Jeff, run in and ask the bartender Marty for a couple of Marlboro Lights. Tell him they are for Darcy.' Into the bar I go, and before I had a chance to find Marty, she and that BMW were long gone. Isn't that a pisser?"

"So, you called Henry?"

"Hell yeah."

Axel knew who Henry was. "That's my personal cab driver, he was taking us out to D.F.W. one afternoon and handed me his card. Let me know if you boys need a ride anywhere. Anywhere, Henry? I had asked. He said, 'If you've got the cash, I'll make the dash!' And, lo and behold, he came and got my sorry ass. Let's get the check before I have to call him again." But not everyone wanted to go.

"Numbers Game," said Axel. "The first time we played this game was here and I lost. It's simple, someone at the table chooses the last three digits on a dollar bill and does not show it to anyone. You go around the table and the first person picks a number from 1 to a 1000. The person who knows the three digits will tell you if the number you chose is high or low. Say 666 is called, and that's low. So the next person picks a number between 667 and 1000 and so on. Whoever picks the number on that hidden bill pays the check. Everyone can lose including the person holding the number."

During Axel's speech, it became apparent that we had finally said something that peaked the girls' interest. "Hold it guys," the blond said. "What kind of game are we playing?"

Once again, Axel took the lead. "It's the numbers game and its for the tab," he said.

"Does that mean our tab as well?" they asked.

"Maybe next time."

"Wait a minute," she said. "We have an idea. Let's play state capitals for both tabs. The table that comes up with a Master List of the most wins, and the losers pay the tab.

Claus chimed in, "Ladies that wouldn't be fair. There are only three of you."

They persisted. "That's mighty kind of you, but we are up for the challenge," said the blonde. "Are you guys?"

A 15 minute time limit was proposed. Like the fools that we were, we engaged. Axel was put in charge of writing the capitals down. Claus, "What the hell is the capital of California for Christ's sake?!"

Springer knew: "Sacramento, write that down, Axel!"

"How are we doing over there boys?" they taunted. Just dandy. In the end, thirty four was all we could come up with. Politely, they stopped at 45. The waiter, aware of the contest by now, brought their check over and placed in front of Springer. "Looks as if they upgraded on the second bottle," he observed. Claus, not too much into wines, asked, "What do you mean upgraded?"

"They went for the Shafer Merlot, a great choice," said the

waiter. "Hell of a lot more money than the Close The Door."

The ladies were getting up to leave, but not before the blond came over to the table. Extending her hand to Axel, she introduced herself. "Hello, my name is Roxanne. It has been a pleasure."

A frustrated Claus wasn't going to allow any more pleasantries between the two. "Rox, is it? Do people call you Rox?"

"Sure," she said, uncertain of what was going on.

"Well, Roxy," he said, "I am just curious. What is it that you have been using on your hair lately? Cheeze Whiz?" I guess we weren't the best losers, but at this particular juncture, Claus was probably entitled to this comment.

The next day at Midway, Sherwin was getting nervous. "Ryan, what's going on with Albany? Has the landlord started his demolition?"

"Yes, last Monday," I responded.

"Well that's not what the guys upstairs tell me," he said. Clavin was always breathing down his neck about The Schedule. What they both failed to realize was Friday's had no control over the timelines of a developer's project and, as a result, they burned a great deal of wasted energy worrying. It was truly pathetic to watch.

To prevent the bullshit from piling up too high, an idea popped into my head. Prior to our Monday development meeting, I would ask that a landlord's representative stand by their phone in case there were any questions that required an answer. For example, each project had a list of comments attached to it that people within the company were assigned to handle. That was fine, but we found that nobody was getting the right answers. The Schedule was full of bullet holes.

Clavin chaired these overly subscribed meetings. "Ok, Albany's next," he began that Monday. "Schedule shows here that we are to open January 30th. Has the landlord started his demolition?"

"Don't think so, no one is returning our calls from his office," someone in the room answered in a diminutive voice.

"Ryan, can you call up there and see what is going on? Put that on the to do list," Clavin ordered.

Not so fast, I thought. "No," I said, "don't put it on the list. We can conference him in right now."

Clavin authoritatively shot back, "No, we have to keep moving here."

I had already expected this type of response. "Clavin," I said, "they are expecting our call." I was already dialing. Squire picked up. "Hello, Squire," I said. "You are on speaker with a whole host of Friday's people wanting to know when you are going to start your demolition."

"Well, I can tell you we have already started and it has been going well. You are coming up for the Liquor License hearing next week?" Squire was on top of things.

"I'll be there with bells on," I said. "Thanks, Squire," and I hung up. We did not always get the answer we wanted to hear, but at least we kept the manure pile to a manageable level.

When I told Buddy that we had the right guy in Houston to call about procuring a helicopter, I wasn't just whistling Dixie. Meet Payton Place who began investing in the drilling of oil wells back in the '70s—a wildcatter of sorts. Payton found great success in this hit or miss field, enabling him to commute back and forth from his home out at Champions in Northwest Houston to his office in Midland Odessa on his private jet. In the late '70s and early '80s he began pouring the proceeds from his oil ventures into commercial tracts of land for the purpose of building much needed shopping centers to support the furious residential growth that was taking place just to the west of Highway 6. When asked, 'Why not stay with oil drilling where you have done so well?' Payton's answer, 'Trees do not grow to the sky."

As was his style with drilling, he jumped in with both feet and built one or two 250,000 square foot generic shopping centers all on speculation. He must have figured retail tenants would not be far behind. The problem was that he wasn't alone. Everyone else was getting in on the act. Developments of all shapes and sizes were sprouting up and the competition for tenants became relentless. What fueled the fire? There was money to lend, an abundance of land to develop and virtually no restrictions as to the type of project you could build.

At Friday's, we initially watched this activity from the sidelines for the simple reason that our Greenspoint location that opened in 1980 was, as Shoe Wagner so aptly described, "sucking air." Hindsight being 20:20, Greenspoint had all the obvious trappings of being a solid producer for us. The market housed millions of square feet of first class office space and a major regional mall was next to be built. There was, however, that one missing ingredient nearest and dearest to our hearts. The residential growth was taking place to the west where there were trees, lakes, and golf course communities. People were commuting to Greenspoint and then going home for the weekend. This Greenspoint deal was baptism under fire. It was supposed to teach the new guys like myself to shy away from deals that are too good to be true, to have the discipline to walk away.

Shoe did not want any part of Northwest Houston. He argued that any body blow, even a light jab, to Greenspoint would certainly take it into negative cash flow territory. It was best to let sleeping dogs lie. Shoe knew he was wrong about the cannibalization issue; this was his polite way of saying that Houston wasn't that great a market for us. If we were going to do anything, he thought we should concentrate on building sales in existing stores.

Payton thought otherwise and once he made verbal contact with us, pursued Friday's with the same ferocity that famed

Houston Oilers defensive end Alvin Bethea pursued quarterbacks. It was at The Astrodome one Sunday when Alvin, after knocking Jim Kelly flat on his back, looked down at the dazed player and said, "I've got to go now, but I'll be back."

Surprisingly, Shoe called me at the bequest of Buddy and asked me when we could schedule a helicopter trip. Shoe was handling this as if a tooth needed pulling. "Ryan, you are busy, I am busy, but let's get this out the way," he told me. "You understand that I am not a huge fan of heights. That's acrophobia, right?"

"Shoe, I promise," I said. "I'll make this short. I can tell you almost to the day I knew I was a scared of heights. My grandparents were taking my sister, brother and I on a motoring tour of Vermont. I was nine years old and we stopped at the foot of The Bennington Monument, a 306 foot high Goliath from where I was standing. Well I didn't know any better. I stepped out on the observation platform with only a metal railing in the way of us landing on a fucking Holstein. When my grandfather took me by the hand, you could hear my screams all the way to Ft. Ticonderoga!" I continued, "Listen Shoe, its only you and I on this ride. There's a helipad at The Hilton on Westheimer. We can meet there." It was agreed.

We watched as Channel 13's helicopter landed. Shoe tried to take comfort in the fact that a TV Station's traffic helicopter was about to fly us around for an hour, saying with a jittery voice, "Nice looking whirlybird. That's not a Bell Jet Ranger is it?"

"No an Aerospatiale," I said, "just like the one we flew around Dallas."

The pilot then got out and greeted us. "You guys must be from Friday's? Payton sends his regards. Listen, hop in and make yourselves comfortable, I'm going to take a piss. Be right back."

This momentary delay gave Shoe more opportunity to get nervous. "Fuck Ryan, this sucks," he said, tensing up. "Trust me Shoe," I said, "You will be fine once we get in the air."

The pilot returned, buckled up and started hitting a few toggle switches, setting the huge blade above us in motion. At that very moment we noticed several flashing lights suddenly appear on the instrument panel. Shoe, looking for any excuse to abort, managed to get out the words, "Told ya Ryan, I do not like these things."

Looks like Shoe's prayers had been answered. "Fellas," the pilot said, "looks like the battery's dead."

Shoe, visibly relieved, assured the pilot that we could just come back another day, but the pilot saw no need. "Stay right here, and we'll be flying in no time," he said somewhat routinely. "Let me grab the bell cap. We can jump start this baby." I chuckled thinking about Claus in Mill Valley with burnt cables. "Glad you think this is funny, Ryan, that Buddy owes me one." We continued to wait for the pilot.

Along came the uniformed Bell Captain driving the pilot in his Ford 150 and stopping at the front of the helicopter. They weren't kidding about the jump start. We sat in the tiny Aerospatiale as we watched them attach the jumper cables.

The sound of the engine cut through Shoe's protestations; the jump start was a success. Our trusty pilot hopped back into the cockpit, and kindheartedly mused, "Beats the shit out of calling Triple A!" We were ready now. The pilot shared his game plan, perhaps to calm Shoe, but it may have made him even more nervous. "Fellas, once we get her going I'll hover to about 50 feet for a few moments just to make sure we are at full power."

We lifted off the ground, Shoe's hopes of further delay dropping off for good. "You guys picked a great day to go flying!" said the pilot with a smile as we made our way up and up and up.

ELEVEN

Huntington

"Know what Blaze, it feels good to be back on New York soil," I said, as we headed for the Hertz counter at La Guardia. It was nice to be home for two weeks, but I found myself getting antsy after a while. "Do you realize I have had a maid coming to the house for six months now and haven't met her yet?" I said to Blaze.

"Oh, the one Sherwin's wife told you to call. You don't have to worry about her. Shit, she may be a born again virgin," Blaze said. "Anyway, did you see that we are staying at The Garden City Hotel? Buddy says it is spectacular!"

"Yeah, we are supposed to show our business cards at the front desk. Something about a special rate."

"It's a hike out to Suffolk County," Blaze said, "and we are going against traffic in both directions. Something about the island, they haven't built any decent hotels."

"Tell me about it." I knew just what he meant. "When I was coming out here in the late '70s, the only place I could find was a Ho Jo's Motor Lodge over near Westbury."

"Oh the one where Connie Francis got raped," recalled Blaze.

"That's the one. She was performing at the Westbury Music Fair that week," I remembered. "How about me, I was staying on the second floor of that rat hole and left the patio door ajar it was so hot. Someone must have noticed it, because the next morning, my watch and money clip were gone. Son of a bitch stacked a couple of milk crate on top of one another and climbed onto my balcony."

"Didn't wake you up?"

"Guess not."

"Ryan, let's head out on the L.I.E., and we can check in later on tonight," Blaze said, formulating the game plan. I started to get the Suffolk County maps out of my briefcase. Friday's had opened in Westbury, so in essence we had Nassau County under wraps. Now if only we could hit the daily double! The legendary basketball coach, Al McGuire once said that if you want to go down Broadway, find yourself players like Butch Lee and Jerome Whitehead. Westbury was our Butch Lee, now we needed to find the likes of Jerome Washington in Suffolk County.

"Ryan, open up that map and let's chart a course. My suggestion is that once we cross into Suffolk County let's traverse the L.I.E. in a north and south direction. The whole island can't be 25 miles wide. Just tell me the exits you want me to get off at. We'll weave a thread back and forth until we have a blanket over this County." That would be the plan.

"I'll be damned," I said suddenly. "I just noticed Plainview on the map. We are coming up on the Oyster Bay Expressway that slices right through it."

"And Plainview is famous for?" Blaze was unsure where I was going with this.

"Cheryl Kopernika."

"Who's she?" Blaze was intrigued.

"We met at The Rusty Scupper in Newport, Rhode Island. May have been eight years ago. Believe it or not she was a Lieutenant in the Navy, a nurse."

"Is that a Polish name?" Blaze asked.

"Good guess. Her parents emigrated from Krakow."

Blaze was confused. "You have met them?"

"Indeed. She was shipped out to San Diego and we always kept in touch, mostly by letter. Then as fate would have it, we reunited here on the island at the time we were building the club in Levittown." I gazed out the window picturing her in my mind. "She had been discharged for a while and was back home. There was a suitor, a Navy Captain, but she was confused, as she put it."

"Ryan," Blaze observed, "they're all confused. You and I are confused." He was right. He continued, "Your old disco days, I remember you telling me a little about it during our interview in Cincinnati." An idea came to him. "Hell, should we stop by this afternoon to see if she is still around? Just kidding, Ryan."

"Your gonna think I'm nuts, but she had a dog with one eye right in the center. One of those caffeine dogs, Pekinese something."

"Oh stop it, you're killing me, the next thing your going to tell me the dog's name was Cyclops."

"There was a great dive bar in East Meadow," I recalled, "owned by a guy named Billy. Can't think of the name of it, but Cheryl and I used to go there. Shit, I'll think of it in a minute. Anyway, the owner Billy used to make the rounds to other joints before stopping back to finish the evening at his place. He was the Pied Piper of Nassau County as it was a popular after work hangout for bartenders, waitresses, and hostesses. A brilliant strategy, since they all had money in there pockets after their shifts, and he stayed open later than anybody else. The cops had to have been looking the other way, though there was never any trouble. Billy didn't come back in his place without notice. He'd walk in, reach over the bar and press a button which shut off the juke box. The regulars knew what was coming next. Blokes like me did not. The owner would yell out "There are only two kinds of people in this place: Fags and Tap Dancers," and with that he would, along with the regulars, start tap dancing. He could then tell who the newcomers were; their feet weren't moving. Then back to the button. By the time the evening wore on he had introduced himself to all that were not tap dancers.

Blaze suggested we stop there on the way back. I promised to try to think of the name of the place. "Get Cheryl off your mind, and it just may come back to you," Blaze cajoled.

"Got it, Dr. Generosity's, that is the name of the place." I looked at the map. "Take Exit 49S."

"It looks like the best residential is sandwiched between The Long Island Sound and the L.I.E., and there is a lot of it," I said as we drove down the ramp.

"It wouldn't surprise me, but let's be patient," Blaze said.
"Republic Airport on the left," I noted.

"Is that where the Grumman Avenger was made?"

"Amityville is where we can turn around and head north," I said. "Fire Island's just off the coast. Always thought it was just Fire Island. Really, there are two islands, East and West. Pretty much for gays is what I hear."

"Wonder why the name is Fire Island."

"How do I mark up Fire Island?"

"Come on, you are the working map specialist."

"OK, put two sets of balls on the map, one on each island."

"Ryan, there are some pretty sexy office buildings up ahead," he noticed.

"Yeah, this will take us on the north side of the L.I.E.. There's Estee Lauder and IBM. Notice how flat the terrain is. These were all potato fields at one point." I was like a tour guide. "Keep going up north. Look at this, Blaze, Old Country Road stretches out this far." I remembered something. "The Friday's In Westbury is just south of Old Country Road. We are coming up on Walt Whitman Mall and Walt Whitman's Birthplace. He was a poet wasn't he, Blaze?"

"Shit if I know," he said.

"Wait a minute," I said, "you can recite half of The Ballad of Reading Jaol, which is what 600 words maybe, and you do not know who Walt Whitman was?"

"We are getting warm here, I can feel it."

"Ah," I noticed, " a Chi Chi's Mexican Restaurant."

"Looks pretty tired if you ask me," Blaze replied. "Ryan, look at how fucked up the parking is? All the way in the back, and the entrance to the restaurant is all the way to the front. Friday's would never lay anything out that poorly."

"Agreed. The guy who did that job had too much Tequila!"

"Either that or it was an old diner location and they had to use the same footprint. Either way, they should have passed on the site," he said. "We will probably get a call on that one. Make a notation: dog with fleas!"

"Blaze, we are coming up to the intersection of Jericho Turnpike and Rte 110. Do you see what I see?"

"God almighty, something is real fishy here." Blaze saw what I saw. "Here we have a vacant piece of property, no sign on it, far enough away from the intersection, bla, bla, bla."

"Look's like she's plenty big enough."

"Someone's going to build an office building. What do you want to bet?" Blaze told me, "Ryan, put a big mark on the map." We might have stumbled on our 100% location right there.

"Take a right on Jericho," I said, as I continued navigating us. "Five miles to the east, then swing south to the L.I.E., and we will head back to Garden City."

"We haven't seen too many apartment complexes out here. Do you ever notice that?"

"Not out this far. This is not exactly part of the five boroughs. Blaze, wait, take a gander over there." I saw something. "We may have spoken too soon. Let's go check it out." One of the best ways to judge the quality of apartment complexes is by the type of cars in the parking lot. If there is a car up on blocks for example, chances are the owner, assuming there is one, will end up working in our kitchen as opposed to being a customer. If there are a lot of cars around during the day, then you may question if anybody living here has a job. Often times we would simply step out of the car and visit the management office. Invariably, someone thinks that you are a prospective tenant, and we could play that role to a tee.

"Good afternoon, may I help you gentlemen?"

Blaze took the lead. "You may, we are looking for a two bedroom apartment and haven't had much luck in finding anything. I'm Blaze and this is my friend Jeff. IBM transfers from Armonk."

"Well guys, isn't that what it stands for; I'll BE MOVED?" he said. "Shell Kasings is the name."

"Nice to meet you Shell. How many apartments are there in the complex?" Blaze asked.

"We have 62 one bedrooms, 12 studios, and 22 two bedrooms, but I'm afraid that there aren't any vacancies at the moment," he said. Now we were getting somewhere. "The influx of corporate tenants in the last year has really been great for our business." Aha. "Listen, I hate to steer you away, but if you get back on the L.I.E. and head west to Exit 57 you will see a new complex under construction called The Colony. You may want to get a deposit down as they are leasing up fast."

"Thanks," we said. "Oh, how about restaurants? Are there any close to where our offices are?"

"You mean like national chains? Not really, unless you call Chi Chi's a restaurant. But, to me, the food sucks and the parking... well, that was an old diner at one time. So, no, unfortunately not." He was a wealth of information, as we expected. He continued, "There has been a sewer moratorium going on with all this new construction. Huntington is swamped with building permits. Someone is going to make a fortune if they can find a location, that is one that the town will approve." A thought came to him. "We did hear that Bennigan's was looking over by The Colony. Have you guys heard of them? My girlfriend said it was a Friday's wan-a-bee."

Blaze picked up, "We've seen them somewhere in our travels haven't we Jeff?" turning to me. "Listen Shell, thanks for the lead. We should get going." M/F 100 was the entry made on our map, and the next day there would be another after our visit to The Colony.

"So, detective Bomberkoff, do you need vectors to Garden City?"

"No, well don't put the map away," he said. "Did you notice the carpet in the management office? You would have to think that the apartments are in a bit of disrepair as well. Definitely not like anything you would see in North Dallas, that's for sure."

"Did I tell you the Axel story about his apartment?" I asked Blaze."We met for drinks at Houston's the other night. He starts telling me how he came home from The Furniture Mart in High Point the other day and detected a really bad odor coming from his apartment. His first reaction was that Mrs. Cartwright in the apartment below had rolled a seven. From what Axel was saying she is a widow in her 80s, and a real nice lady. Sadly, he called the management office to inform them that they may want to look in on her. Wouldn't you know it he said she opened the door."

"She pulled a Lazarus on him," said Blaze, "back from the dead."

"No kidding," I continued. "Now he thought he'd give a look see in the kitchen. Shit, I'd bet money that he couldn't turn on a stove with out having to read the directions. Hell, we were at his mother's house for Thanksgiving and she asked him to set the table. After completing this menial task he parked his ass on the couch. She comes out of the kitchen asking us who's left-handed? Anyway, back to the weird smell, he peered into his own microwave, and could see that he had left an uncooked chicken breast inside. He said he had to shut the door it smelled so bad. He unplugged the fucker, gingerly carried the maggot infested microwave down the stairs and tossed it into the dumpster. Apparently, the ever curious and observant Mrs. Cartwright watched this all unfold, and ran out to ask 'Oh dear, did you just throw a microwave away?'"

We put away the map and sat back for the rest of the ride back to the hotel. Road warriors like us do not need maps to find airports or hotels. Like bloodhounds, we have a keen sense of where they are. (It's like pressing forward in the drivers seat to look up for airplanes just to make sure that you are heading in the right direction, but a little more instinctive than that.)

"Garden City Hotel, Blaze, go right on 7th Street," I said. "See the Cupola?" The original hotel was built in 1874, and at the time we checked in it had under gone a major refurbishment.

"Good evening, gentleman. Do you have reservations?"

"Yes, Bomberkoff and Ryan. T.G.I.Friday's."

"I see. Buddy Busch from your company was here last week. The first night we opened in fact."

"Yes, he was telling us how lovely it was." Looking across the street, I pointed. "The train station across the street. How long a ride into Manhattan?"

"Oh not long, 45 minutes or so."

Blaze caught on. "Ryan, no, let's use some restraint. Let's meet at the bar in twenty minutes." So be it. Blaze and I decompressed at the hotel bar and decided to have dinner right where we sat. We hadn't even thought about lunch that day, but that was par for the course.

Where the practice began, I am not sure, but in those days

on the Island it was an unwritten rule for bartenders to "buy you a drink" after you had kept them company for a while. This became a major concern of ours in Westbury and it took some time to mold the right team. The staff that remained were the ones smart enough to realize that volume solves everything and the giveaways were not worth the consequences: an automatic firing. Go work the horse barns next door at Roosevelt Raceway if you like.

"We got a little twinge in Huntington today," Blaze said.

"Yeah," I replied. "Tomorrow we'll finish the map and check out the evening business. That is a big-time market out here for sure."

"Is that night club you built still open in Levittown? What was the name of it?"

"Uncle Sam's. Yes it is, but it has since changed hands," I said. I could remember it like yesterday. "Blaze, it was The Studio 54 of Long Island, the hottest thing going. Shit, we promoted a manager trainee from our club in Davenport, Iowa thinking he was an "Honest Abe." Well he wasn't there six months until he decided to take off with the weekend receipts. He got $34,000 in cash. That was the beginning of the end." I took a sip of my drink.

Over lunch Dalton told us that a while back he thought that one of the primary reasons for Friday's success was attributable to the Polygraph Test.

That's right. At the beginning of the venture, people warned that in this business employees will steal from you any chance they get. If that isn't bad enough, drug use will become a prevalent factor. A test was designed and implemented especially for Friday's and at first the employees balked at such a bold move. At about the sametime, thirty employees from Steak and Ale were fired over a theft ring that involved everyone from the front door to the dishwasher. Apparently everyone was recieving a $25.00 bonus after each shift. Five of the ringleaders approached us about the operation in hopes of getting a job with Friday's. This repenting did not help their cause with Friday's, however, it did restore emloyee confidence in the system. The company was looking for the best of the best. From that day forward this even playing field elevated the standards by which they operated.

"Well Blaze, what do you say we call it an evening!"

"Ryan, grab me a coffee and I'll bring the car around front," Blaze said.

"Let's take the southern route to Suffolk County this morning shall we?" I said.

"Now I know why New Yorkers refer to the Long Island Expressway as the biggest lie in the world." Navigating our way through the well kept streets of Garden City, we could see why this was an attractive place to live. Manhattan beckoned you to take the short train trip into Penn Station. Jump on the Hempstead line and let the LIRR do the driving! You could really have the best of both worlds – city and country.

"The Southern State Parkway is the ticket," Blaze said, after we'd been driving for a little while. "It will take us to The Sunken Meadow where we can head back north. What did you call it yesterday? The weave?" We had our driving plan for the day. "Ryan, by the way, you didn't piss in the bidet did you?"

"Is that what that contraption is called? That's a first for me," I admitted. "You know I was going to ask the housekeeper in the hallway what the hell it was. The French come up with that did they?"

"You would think," Blaze replied. "Well, you know that any guy that comes back to the room whiskeyed is going to think that he's pissing in the toilet. Whoops!" We shared a laugh thinking of that image." The housekeepers couldn't have been happy when they saw those being installed."

"We want Exit 41N. It's a ways, but it looks like clear sailing. Oh," I remembered something. "Leaves of Grass was the book of poems that put Walt Whitman on the map."

Stunned, Blaze replied, "Where'd you find that out? What did you do, sneak back down to the bar last night and chat it up with our favorite bartender? He seemed to have a wealth of knowledge."

"No," I said, "I called the B.P.L."

"The B.P.L.?"

"The Boston Public Library, 617-536-5400. I have the number committed to memory." He couldn't believe it. I continued, "I do the same with Boston Globe Sports 617-929-3235. If you want a trivia question answered, especially if there is a small wager involved, keep those two numbers handy. Hell, I called The L.A. Public Library once because the B.P.L. was closed."

"And what did you need answered?"

"The longest river in the world," I said.

"Got to be the Amazon isn't it?" he wondered.

"Nope, it's the Nile," I answered. "It's 3200 and something miles, I believe was the correct answer."

"Interesting."

"Now," I continued, "of course The Boston Globe Sports desk is open all hours, but they aren't always as receptive to satisfying dumbass questions. One guy over at Ballsonly Golf Club had a question about Fenway Park. He wanted to know when the last time a relief pitcher was ferried to the mound in a golf cart."

"Shit, I remember they used to do that. What year did they discontinue that practice?"

"Don't know, as soon as I asked the question, you could hear a click!" Well, they weren't a trivia service after all.

Blaze, looking up, observed, "There is some traffic up ahead. Maybe we should take the Wantagh."

"Nah, keep going. It will clear out at some point anyway.

My Aunt Dottie lives in Wantagh, on Duckpond Road," I said. "What a pisser, drives one of those Plymouth Magnums. Not sure what is under the hood but the fucker just flies. She drives it up to North Quincy to visit my father."

"Good for her," said Blaze.

"The car is a dark green color with very few markings on it, no 390 on the side like my fathers LTD. It's the perfect car," I mused, "to pull up at a red light next to some punk that thinks he's hot stuff driving his mother's Camaro convertible."

Blaze picked right up on this. "Your aunt," he said, "is driving what we refer to in Erie, Pennsylvania as a "fuck you car."

"Oh, yeah? How's that?" I asked.

"That's when you turn your head to look at the other driver, knowing that as soon as the light turns green you are going to leave him in the dust!"

"So you don't have to say a thing, the look says it all," I nodded.

"Shit, Ryan, I had a GTO, Gas Tires And Oil, and it was pretty much the same drill. No one in Erie could touch me and there were a lot of muscle cars that tried. Your Aunt Dottie must have had to stop at every single gas station on the way up to Boston, unless she took the ferry from Port Jeff."

"No that's northeast of Huntington, she wouldn't have done that. It'd be a waste of her time, especially in that monster. You don't drive that car, you aim it."

"So, how'd a nice girl from Quincy end up in New York anyway?" Blaze asked me.

"Married a guy from Queens, my Uncle Bill. She met him back home at The Clam Box on Wollastan Beach."

"The Clam Box?"

"Ya, we should stop there on our Boston trip. If you enjoy clams, this is the spot.... Anyway, this was back when WWII was getting cranked up and Bill was stationed for a while at Squantum Naval Air Station on the other side of the bay where they grew up. He was a yeoman in the Navy and eventually would end up in the same PT boat Squadron as J.F.K. himself. I could talk your ear off about this all day, because there is a lot of history there with my father and his brothers' involvement in the war and all, but it was at Cousin Butch's wedding, which incidentally was held pretty close to where we are going, that after many years of wanting to know, an opening presented itself where the question could be asked. The handsome son of a gun was off in the corner stoking his pipe (that he never seemed to be without). That's when I approached him. 'Uncle Bill, forgive me for asking as I know that you may not want to talk about it, but I read about PT 109, and I was wondering, were you there when J.F.K. was rescued near The Solomon Islands?' Well, he took one or two puffs on his pipe and looked me straight in the eye with those baby blues of his and said 'Yes. We were determined to find him. The crews all knew what a terrific swimmer he was, so we knew there was a good chance that he was out there somewhere. It took us 24 hours or so but, thanks to the guy upstairs, we found him.'"

"Must have had a special admiration for J.F.K., your aunt and uncle," Blaze said.

"Oh yeah. During her visits to the old homestead in Quincy, Aunt Dottie would recount many stories, her favorite being the ticker tape parade for J.F.K. in New York. Uncle Bill was working on Wall Street at the time and, lo and behold, the then President Kennedy recognized Bill waving to him from the sidewalk. The story goes that J.F.K. directed the Secret Service to haul Bill's ass up into the car."

"No kidding," Blaze said in wonderment.

"Sure as hell," I said. "She would also say that she only saw her husband cry twice. Once, the day Cousin Butch left the house to join the Navy, and the other upon learning about the death of J.F.K."

"Well, I'll bet. Great story, Ryan," said Blaze. "We've got to make sure we get to The Clam Box." He looked out the window. "We are coming up on Exit 41."

Blaze is really something. He was a joy to be with as were Claus, Bewly and Sherwin. Not everyone you work with would be an ideal person to spend time riding in the car with. Honestly, these guys could drive cross country with me and I'd be happy.

Three of my high school buddies made the drive during a summer break stopping in Buffalo to pay a visit. They pulled into our club parking lot in a blue Chevy Malibu that had a large wooden box strapped to the roof. We surmised that their belongings were inside. Hand painted on the side of this box for the entire world to see was a sign. It read: DON'T LAUGH - YOUR DAUGHTER MAY BE IN HERE. You just have to imagine what a farmer is thinking watching those three characters driving through Kansas.

Back on the L.I.E., I snapped out of my daydream. "Blaze, take the next exit, that looks like a fairly decent size apartment complex." I directed us through a few turns, thinking we were coming upon a goldmine, but it turned out to be a false alarm. Just a psychiatric hospital and that wouldn't do for this purpose. "Let me mark that on the map, Ha Ha Hotel. Take a right on Commack Road. This will take us north to the Long Island Sound." I really did know my way around here. "You know, Blaze," I said, thinking out loud. "Hauppauge just may be another market for us in a few years. It lies east of where we are now and our 100% is 5 miles or so in the other direction. Sorry did not mean to jump to any conclusions, I just thought of it."

"Good boy, Ryan. You may be right. When we make our first stop somewhere we can take another look see on the map. It is always good to recap after a while."

"You mean we are going to stop for lunch?" I asked, dumbfounded.

Blaze, now stopped at a red light had time to peer down at my markings. "Ryan," he said, "when we get back to Dallas, let me show you how a real mapping job is done."

"Yeah, look at this," I said. "See all the residential north of Jericho Turnpike. Goodness gracious, there's a bunch of them here."

"And, they all have to head south to get on the L.I.E., don't they?" Blaze asked.

"Light's green," I told him. We kept going.

"Have you been to Friday's in Atlanta," Blaze asked me.

"Yes, at The Prado on Roswell Road, you mean. Busier than dog shit when we there."

"Pay close attention," said Blaze. Although no one foresaw what would happen after 11 years of doing a box office business, our location had split into two markets. Shit, the handwriting was on the wall. Sales had been on the decline for some time. "Something to be cognizant of when you go through the mapping exercise," Blaze observed.

"Yes, as you look at Huntington in particular there are similarities as Roswell Road ran north to south. Didn't it?" I couldn't exactly remember. "Now, let's hug the coastline of Long Island Sound until we hit Route 110. Our blanket is just about finished," I said, looking up from the map.

"Why don't we shoot over to Hackensack in the morning. You can see a Friday's under construction," Blaze said.

"That would be neat," I agreed. We spent so much time in the car and on the road, that seeing a new Friday's would be a welcome change of pace. The car took on a submarine like quiet as we stealthily headed south on Route 110 towards Jericho Turnpike. "This last leg will tell us if we in have fact have found the bulls eye," I said.

Our last order of business was to jot down some contact information on the map. Let's see, Reckson Associates. "Blaze, will you read that number out to me? Thanks."

"Ryan, why do I think you'll be coming back here often and soon," Blaze pondered. "You've got some serious follow up work to do."

Friday morning we were off to Hackensack, pretty much a straight shot over the GW Bridge. Bridge crossings give me the heavie-jeavies. From my slumped position, I can see the joggers on the bridge and the people walking across. Has the thought ever crossed their minds that the person behind them could all of sudden decide to give them the heave-ho over the railing? Why do people tempt fate like that? Odds are slim, but these are the things a true acrophobic thinks about.

We reached Hackensack and were greeted outside by Colt Hammer, Friday's Construction Manager. Colt gave us the heads up that Clavin had been in town for a few days and was inside exerting his powers over everyone. "Careful boys," he warned, "The Commandant is in there grandstanding." Colt, like us, would fly back and forth on a regular basis. We were sure to see him at LaGuardia later on in the day. "Stick around, boys, there are going to be some fireworks. Look over yonder. See the chubby guy in the light grey shark-skin suit getting out of that two door Delta 88, the one with the opera windows in the back? He is going in to have a little chat with our man. You see that 24 yard dumpster at the side of the building? Clavin finds a trash hauler out of the Yellow Pages. That's all fine and dandy, but there's a problem."

"What's the problem?" Blaze asked.

"Well, up here the trash business is territorial," Colt answered. "They are like lions. You just can't walk in off the plains and expect to join the pride. We tried to explain this to Clavin, but the idiot won't listen. Come on in and watch this circus act. You picked a good day to stop by."

As soon as Clavin saw us, he put on this air of 'look who's

in charge!' Standing close enough, we could all hear the rather polite conversation.

"Clavin, Guido Iacavelli," he introduced himself. "Quite an undertaking you've got going on here. You'll knock 'em dead." Handing Clavin his business card, he said, "We just stopped by to tell you that my company handles the trash service in this part of town. No biggie, we realize that you guys are from what, Texas? The price is the same and we'll give you great service."

Clavin, of all things, tried to dispatch this guy all in our presence. "That's quite all right, Guido," he began. "We are all set. My construction manager here will call you if we need you." He passed Guido's card to Colt, a not-so-subtle sign that it didn't mean much to him.

Guido was not going to argue; he didn't have to. "Well if that is what you say, have a nice day." It was within the hour that two large trucks arrived, followed by Guido driving the Delta 88. The first truck removed the 24 yarder that was there and the second truck slipped in its replacement. It was a hoot to watch. Clavin was trying his best to pretend he did not notice what was taking place, but he wasn't fooling anyone.

In fact, it would have been the perfect time for Clavin to show his true colors. "Well," he could have said. "I guess he showed me." But, he just couldn't muster up enough courage to do it. Taking that as our cue to leave, we got back into the car and said goodbye to the crew.

"Blaze, 212 foot clearance at the center of the G.W."

"You didn't see me use the pay phone did ya? Keep your eyes on the walkway. Ryan, maybe you can tell me if anyone gets thrown over the railing."

"Very funny. Let's see if we can make the 1 o'clock out of La Guardia."

"We want The Triborough don't we?"

"Yup. How about that Clavin?"

"Way too serious for my blood."

We were able to get on the earlier flight, which was terrific as I could now spring my dog loose from Toothacres kennel, where he'd been staying for days now. It pained me to leave him all the time, not so much because of his advancing age, but more for the lack of exercise. Fortunately, the kennel had a terrific handler on duty and Colonel was walked on a daily basis. Irish setters, like all sporting dogs, require a great deal of exercise, so I'd make sure we made up for lost time on the weekends. Blaze, a pet owner himself, asked me about him on the flight back.

"So how's The Colonel?"

"He's doing fine. Just a little blip on the radar screen. The vet scraped off a cancerous growth on his leg. Found it while brushing his coat. We can only hope that it hadn't spread."

"How long has he been with you anyway?"

"Thirteen years," I said proudly. "We've been everywhere together. He used to wag his tale every time we passed a Holiday Inn sign. Knoxville, Buffalo, Detroit, Rhode Island, Cincinnati, where he was born, Boston, where my mother and sister baby-sat for him. All great stuff. He's even a father. It is amazing how they get the scent; somehow he found a female Irish setter in heat a mile or so from my mom's house. Apparently after several overtures at this owner's doorstep, it was decided that they should spend the weekend together. I remember that Sunday night I came to pick him up. I'm not sure if he wanted to come home with me or not! Practically had to carry him to the car he was so exhausted!"

"No kidding," said Blaze.

"Why can't his master experience a weekend like that?" I wondered, Blaze laughing at the thought. "Hackensack will be your fourth opening won't it, Blaze?"

"Indeed it will be," he said. "Willow Grove was my first." He started thinking about the past. "Truly an amazing company, Ryan.

Look at the time and money they have invested in us. In your case, what will it have been now before the Albany opening?"

"Two years and 9 months," I responded, precisely recalling the timing.

"Oh so you're keeping track?" Blaze chuckled.

"Yes, of course," I laughed along with him. "But, seriously, they don't happen overnight like some people would think, do they?"

"Ryan," he agreed, "if only people knew. But hey. Let them think what they want to think. As long as we win every time we tee it up."

"So, Blaze, are you concerned about this year?" I asked. "Do you think twenty is too many?"

"Two times too many if you ask me." I sighed. I was afraid I wasn't the only one who thought this. Blaze continued, "It is taking too long for the ship to leave the harbor. What I mean by that, Ryan, is that the results aren't there at the beginning, not the whole first six months mind you. No, it's taking a year or longer for the new restaurants to find their groove."

"A year is just too long," I agreed.

"The good news," Blaze said, "is they are finding their groove in the end for sure. After all, Viken and Buddy and the rest know what they are doing. The bad news is that Wall Street does not have the patience." How right he was. We would find that out in the months to come.

By the time Monday afternoon rolled around we knew more and more about Huntington. Reckson, the major first class office developer, was looking forward to meeting with us, though there were major hurdles to overcome with respect to free-standing restaurants.

These hurdles made the vacant piece on Route 110 all the more attractive. Who owned it? We finally found out: a family trust under the name Hiho Silver LTD. Our contact was Harry

Fabbiano, a real estate consultant for a Manhattan lawyer representing the family. Harry did not sound too optimistic about the prospects for a restaurant there, but he was willing to arrange a meeting with us at the end of the week.

"Welcome back to the Garden City Hotel, Mr. Ryan," always a nice touch when you are greeted with your name. After inquiring about the train schedule, I sat in the lobby to rehearse my "tell the story" speech that was scheduled for 4p.m. that afternoon. Harry had briefed me on the phone as best he could about Linus Argente, the trust's lawyer: a confirmed bachelor, late fifties, only on rare occasions would he leave Manhattan and even then he couldn't recall when that was, shopped the men's department at Bergdorf Goodman, and he would keep you waiting.

Linus's office was at 1290 Avenue of the Americas, so there was plenty of sightseeing to do during the twenty or so blocks to midtown. I blended right in with the crowd, walking down the streets, just me and my briefcase. My mind got sidetracked a bit, but that was okay, as there was plenty of time to kill and it's never a good idea to peak too early. Best to save your best for game time.

The sight of Madison Square Garden brought back memories of my first trek into the city in 1970. The semi-finals of the NIT basketball tournament pitting Marquette against L.S.U., or how about Dean Meminger against Pistol Pete Maravich. That evening four us of piled into one room at The Roosevelt Hotel. There was only one bed in the room and before anyone could draw straws, one smart individual peed on the bed, turned to us, and said, 'I guess I know where I am sleeping.' Crafty move or just plain disgusting? Either way, it worked. Must be an old Indian trick.

Before long, I reached the Avenue of the Americas and found the office. Harry's forewarning about the wait served me well.

You often wonder in these situations whether arriving late will reduce your wait time or whether the wait time begins at your arrival, regardless of when it is. In this case, it was the latter.

There was a spectacular globe standing at one end of the conference room. Linus's travels perhaps were completed vicariously through this worldly artifact. "Hello, Jeff. I am Linus Argente, welcome to New York," he came in, shaking my hand. Again, Harry was spot on. Linus could have done a photo shoot for the cover of GQ, right then and there. Have him stand next to the globe with the New York skyline in the background, and bingo. He made quite the impression on me.

"I was just admiring your globe."

"Yes, it was a gift from an attorney friend of mine in Rome," he replied. "Please sit down." There was a split second where he was making a slight adjustment to his suit coat that gave me an opening.

"Linus, allow me to spend a few minutes to tell you about our company, the roots of which you may already know. Friday's began here in Manhattan in 1965." At that moment he reached over with his left arm to put a halt to the proceedings.

"Jeff, does your company have any debt?" he wanted to know. Shame on me for not knowing, though he may nonetheless have appreciated my answer.

"Linus," I replied, "we do. However, I do not know the details."

Happy to have him steal my thunder, as it surely stopped me from shoveling any deeper, he picked up. "Jeff, Hiho Silver LTD does not have any. A 13-year-old lovely girl from a very prominent Long Island family is counting on my firm to insure that her future is secure. Her father crashed his Lamborghini into a tree on Montauk Highway killing both himself and his wife in the process." He continued, "to give you an idea, we invest in companies like Exxon-Mobil, Proctor and Gamble, you get the picture. We certainly don't have a record of investing in flamboyant restaurant companies." Sounded like the door was closed. "That being said," he continued, "the fact that we are not going to do a deal with Friday's will not preclude us from having a drink together. If you will kindly indulge me for a moment, please help yourself to the phone."

Linus did not say where we were going, but it was an enjoyable walk. He intimated that he and Harry Fabbiano had known each other since their childhood days in Brooklyn, received his law degree from Columbia and worked for a while in the criminal justice system for Attorney General Bobby Kennedy. This man had some stories to tell, and it was over drinks at the Columbus Citizens Committee that he was going to tell them. He chose to sit by one of several fireplaces in this converted Brownstone. Sinking comfortably into a leather chair, Linus ordered for the both of us, "Jimmy, open those Bombay Doors!" Could this be my second mistake of the day? Gin? That juniper berry can get a person into trouble. (A reformed gin drinker once told me there wasn't a month that didn't go by where he'd lose either a fight or a raincoat.)

Well the second martini loosened us both up and Linus's softer underbelly appeared. "Ryan, there used to be outstanding flesh in that Friday's on First Avenue," he began. Trying to fit bits and pieces of our story back into the conversation was going to be difficult. I would try nonetheless. "Linus, you should see our restaurant in Westbury. It's the flagship of the fleet."

"Jeff, six years ago next month will be the last time that I left the city. That was to meet some stiff from Briarcliff who thought he was good enough to marry my sister. Another one of those guys born on third base—the asshole was wearing green pants with red lobsters. I knew right then and there he was the wrong guy."

The Bombay had me on the ropes, but I was able to regain my footing. I didn't want to lose control of the conversation.

"Linus," I persevered, "we could be a tenant of yours for twenty to twenty-five years, perhaps longer," I said.

"Our site is that good?" he asked. He was interested. I had him.

"Your site is that good," I assured him.

"Ryan, you seem like a talented guy," he said. "Why are you working for Friday's?"

"If you are going to work for somebody, why not work for the best?" I replied.

"Jimmy, order us two veal chops and bring a bottle of Brunello di Montalcino."

"Excellent, Sir, your table will be ready in a moment."

We clanged wine goblets and launched into the Brunello.

"Ryan," he started. "What, they don't teach you how to drink wine at Friday's? Hold the stem like it's a feather, not an axe. When you touch glasses you will hear a ping not a thud. Here, try it again." Ping. Hey, I figured, whatever it took to win him over.

The Veal chops arrived along with a second bottle of wine. "A toast: Acqua Fresca, Vino Puro, Fica Stretta, Cazzo Duro."

"Should I ask for a translation?"

"That would break the flow. Listen, speak with Harry Fabbiano. He is like a brother to me and I trust him with my life. Where are you staying?"

"The Garden City Hotel."

"Never heard of it." He must be busting my chops, I thought. But, let it be. After a round of Sambucas, he hailed a cab. I thanked him and headed to Penn Station. It was a great evening. I figured Harry Fabbiano had to be as solid as Linus, considering their history together.

Soon after, Harry drove out from his office in Queens to meet me on site. To compare Harry with Linus is easy. Harry has the disheveled look, Linus does not. Driving a weathered four door Black Fleetwood Harry, pulled up in what is called a "Real Estate Car." Big ass engine, comfortable to ride in, and most importantly it can take a body blow. It was the Bismarck on wheels.

"Ryan, you charming devil you. Not too many people get as far as the dinner table with Linus."

"Harry," I said, "I've got to wonder, you must have heard the toast before?" I repeated parts I remembered to him.

"So the Bombay doors were open I see. He was toasting to tight pussys and hard cocks."

"Beautiful."

Harry got right down to business. "Ryan, just like you I don't need the practice so let me give it to you straight. There is plenty of room for your restaurant to fit on this site along with an office building, but zoning will only permit one structure and the highest and best use is an office building. It is simply a numbers game. Don't bother asking about a variance. We can't talk about an in-line space on the first floor because we are going with parking on that level. Parking that you could use at night, I might add. My wife and I spend a lot of time in your Westbury location. Even she says you would kill out here."

"Harry, may I take this site plan back to Dallas with me. There are some talented people that may have an off the wall idea or two."

"Be my guest, however, unless its going on the roof, I don't see how we can pull it off."

"Let me get back to you on Monday. Thanks again for coming all the way out here to meet with me. Oh, Harry, is there a stock aerial that you can send to me?"

"Sure, I'll send it out tonight."

Back at Headquarters, Scooter started stalking the large site plan spread out on the conference room table. "Jeff, how's Colonel doing?" Scooter had just gotten a chocolate lab puppy and was taking him to the same veterinarian.

"Doing okay, took him out to Lake Lewisville on Sunday," I said. Never would we bring Scooter a reduced copy of a site plan; it was always the largest we could find.

"It must be important if real estate thought enough to bring me a plan with such scope."

"Only the best for our man Scooter."

"Well Jeff, unless we put this fucker on the roof, I don't know," he said.

"Look," I pointed, "there is plenty of room for both buildings and their parking scheme is brilliant."

Scooter began mumbling. "Now how do we become one building to satisfy the town? Jeff, have you been to Gershwin's on Walnut Hill?"

"Next to the office building? Yeah, we've been down there. Nice touch with the baby grand piano!"

"Well you probably would not notice, but, although it appears to be a free standing restaurant, I believe part of the structure is attached to the office building. Now even if it isn't, there may be a way to accomplish this in Huntington. How about if we run a steal beam or two from our roof to their building?" Scooter started drawing a series of sketches. "Or, better still," he said, "a covered walkway."

"Will that qualify as one structure?" I asked.

"It's a long shot, but it just might work," he said.

"Scooter boy, let me put a man on it," I said. Harry was street smart, the perfect man to find out if we were onto something. Scooter's schematic plan had merit and with some tweaking, the town became more and more receptive to the idea. Our success in Westbury was clearly a catalyst. The more Huntington got involved, the more they wanted Westbury East. They felt that this was the right site as there were not any sewer moratoriums to deal with in this part of town.

Linus remained on the sidelines and relied on Harry to hammer out a deal. Harry accommodated us on just about everything we asked for, with the exception of the Base Rent. Linus wanted a higher premium and for all intents and purposes he was justified in asking for it. There was nothing earth-shattering about their request. This was not a swing-high-swing-low style, pile-on-the-bullshit-type of negotiation. This was between two entities that have decided to do business with each other: the best kind.

In speaking with Blaze about the deal he knew we had done the best we could. "Run it on the Lotus 1 2 3 and see what the I.R.R. [internal rate of return] shows. Ryan, increase the construction costs by 15%, that's going to be a union job; and plug in a sales volume slightly above our national average. Where is Sherwin on all this? We are about to cash a daily double ticket."

Sherwin walked into our office with the Letter of Intent. "Fellas, the Base Rent is $25,000 too high. We should go back to these guys."

"Sherwin," I said, "we have done the best that we could. I would not recommend doing that, since it may open up a large can of worms. You have no idea what we have been through to get to this point."

Blaze came to my defense. "Ryan's right on this one, Sherwin. Besides, this is Westbury East, not Northwest Houston. "Ryan, who is this guy Harry Fabbiano anyway?"

"Oh, he is a real estate consultant for Linus Argente."

Sherwin asked if we could set up a meeting with Linus. He was becoming overbearing. "Suppose we can, Sherwin. Even if we could, it could be counterproductive. Let me advise against it."

Sherwin wouldn't quit. "Boys, I have a fiduciary responsibility to the company to see that we have made the best deal possible. Let's fly up there up and get after it." Blaze thought that Sherwin had lost what little grip he had on the wheel.

A MAN SHORT

Exasperated, Blaze formed a circle with the thumb and forefinger of his right hand and held it up for Sherwin to see. "Sherwin, do you know why a sperm whale's throat is this large?"

A perplexed Sherwin, "No, why?"

"'Cause that's the way it is."

Soon after, Betty copied us on a letter he wrote to Linus in advance of our meeting. It was too late to intercept as it had already been picked up for delivery. Harry's admonishments fell on deaf ears. The meeting was set for 4p.m. on a Wednesday.

Sherwin had a bounce in his step the entire way from Penn Station to 52nd Street. He was brimming with confidence, or perhaps was he just feeding off the energy of New York. "Sherwin, we can relax in the conference room, Linus will be fashionably late."

"Nice looking globe," Sherwin admired.

Just then Linus walked in. "You like that? It spins 21° on it axis," he said, holding out his hand. "You must be Sherwin Bliss." Linus motioned for us to sit down with the scrolled up letter from Sherwin. He allowed Sherwin to proselytize but only briefly. "Sherwin," he began, "your letter has reminded me that perhaps the family trust does not have such a good deal. Harry has been instructed to increase the rent by an additional $25,000 per year and incorporate that into a new agreement. Now if you will excuse me gentlemen." He was finished. There were not going to be any 'I told you so' or 'see what I meant.' We decided to walk back to Penn Station.

In the end, Huntington opened in May of 1986. The first part of my prediction to Linus has already come true as the restaurant enters its 24th year in business.

TWELVE

Jersey

Barry Feedlot and Jeff Bussman, two highly respected Real Estate brokers from Deal, New Jersey, were listening intently as I outlined our growth plans for their home turf, Monmouth County. There was an ICSC Weekend Conference going on in Manhattan and we had decided to meet in the lobby of The New York Hilton.

Fortunately for myself and Friday's, a little elf by the name of Bill Harbinger was eavesdropping in on our conversation. The three of us were sitting on one of two back to back couches, and although Bill went unnoticed, I was soon to find out he was perched over my shoulder well within earshot of our conversation. Incredible when you look back at what transpired from this fortuitous meeting.

Gathering the Friday's information that was spread out on the coffee table, I soon heard a voice from the other couch. "Excuse me, I couldn't help but overhear your conversation with the gentlemen that just left. You must be with T.G.I.Friday's." He came around to greet me. I invited him to sit. He introduced himself, and I introduced myself. He handed me his business card, and I saw he was General Counsel for Levin Management of Plainfield, New Jersey.

"You are an attorney?" I asked.

"Yes, by trade," he replied. "Jeff, we own Blue Star Shopping

Center on Route 22 in Watchung. Are you familiar with it?"

"Not yet, I am just getting my arms around the entire market, actually."

"Yeah, you are looking at a site in Princeton and Eatontown where those guys were from. Deal is a lovely town." He had listened to our entire chat.

"So you were listening?" I asked.

"Your voice carries," he said.

"So I'm told," I admitted. "One of my golfing buddies had my name on my golf bag tag changed to Captain Loud, if that tells you anything."

My first impression of Bill was a good one. Just something about the manner in which he spoke told me he was a good guy.

"Are you staying in New York, Jeff?"

"Yes, we are at The Essex House."

"You should try and take a look while you are here. We are just on the other side of the Hudson maybe twenty- five miles from where we are sitting," he said.

"What should I look for Bill?" I asked.

"Go take a look and if you like the market we can figure something out," he said.

Could this be another Albany, I wondered? Sunday would be a good day to go. "I'll call you at the beginning of the week either way," I promised.

That concluded my lobby business. Now it was off to meet some people at The Oak Bar at The Plaza Hotel. The site of Central Park made me chuckle. It was during one of the New York City marathons that the leaders had reached Central Park South when I noticed a guy dressed as The Cape Crusader running through the park in their direction. One could only guess that he wanted to escort the leaders to the finish line. N.Y.P.D. got sight of him and took pursuit. Batman left the panting cops in the dust, hurdled the barricade and hit the afterburners as he had some catching up to do. The last cop that gave up yelled, "Ok, you win, just don't trip anybody!"

Ben Springer and Preston Hollow were at the bar when I arrived. Surely there would be others as this was a well attended conference. After all, you don't get many chances to visit New York City on the bubble. The place can burn a hole in your pocket if you want to do it right.

Ben laid a fifty on the bar for eight Heinekens and was shy by fourteen dollars not counting the tip. "This is New York," we could hear the bartender say. "Ryan, is that Payton Place, The Houston developer walking this way?" asked Springer.

"Shit, he noticed me. He has been bugging me about Willowbrook."

"Out by Champions?"

Too late, he was there. "Hello, Jeff, Goddamn it's good to see you," he led off with. "I am prepared to sweeten the pot in Houston if you guys can move quickly. Payton, my friend—let's keep an eye on developments out there if we can; who knows, we just may do something someday. How about dinner this evening?"

"My friends and I really hadn't planned anything," I said, "just going with the flow." I introduced Payton to Preston and Springer. "Howdy! How about the 21 Club? Dinner's on me," he said. "Ben, Preston, how about it? We can make it a foursome. Tell you what, it feels like Houston outside, let me hunt down a limo and I'll be back to pick you guys up. Friday night in the Big Apple and a big conference in town?"

"If you insist."

Three Heinekens later (and that's three each making it nine times eight dollars equaling seventy two dollars), Payton returned. Preston glanced at the bar tab and removed a honeybee from his money clip. "Men, Fame and Fortune may leave you, but thirst is eternal."

"Boys, our car is ready. Come on, let's go," I said.

"You guys have to be famished," Payton said. He was right about that. What a thrill. The 21 Club. "Ever been, Ryan?" asked Ben. "No," I said, "just glad we're not playing the numbers game for the check."

A relic of a limo was waiting outside on Central Park South. Preston, half joking, asked, "Payton, how many payments do you think he has left on this chariot?"

"Shit, the concierge had to call across the river," he said. "There was nothing available in the city." To make matters worse, the windows were at half mast; the AC wasn't working. The ride to 21 West 52nd Street was going better than expected, however, our luck was soon to run out a mere two blocks from the restaurant's front door. The old geezer of a limo rebelled as the traffic slowed to a crawl. First the warning lights, then the distinct smell of radiator fluid. "Ryan," Ben said, "she's ready to blow if she hasn't already." Then we stalled, and it was almost as if a maestro was standing on the hood looking back down the one way street, giving the nod to the horn section—car horns that is—to start blasting away. The sounds echoed off the Brownstones. It was utter chaos. Payton, like an embattled tank commander asked the crew for advice, Springer, "Let's pay the poor bastard and walk the rest of the way."

We ducked inside The 21 Club but not before the maitre'd made a slight adjustment to my tie. "There you go sir, now you look handsome." Welcome to The 21 Club, I guess. Payton asked for the wine list. "Jeff," he said, "how the hell will they ever get that car off the street?" Ah don't worry, one of those giant Sikorsky's will fly in and hoist it right out of there! Come on Payton, lighten up—I'm just kidding. A dejected Payton commented, "Jeff, my stars might not be lined up, first the dead battery in the chopper and now this." Now with both of us holding a glass of Morgan Sauvignon Blanc, I said something that brought a smile to his face. "Payton, may all your problems be that small."

A MAN SHORT

Payton appointed Preston spokesperson for the table. "Will you bring us the Seafood Platter, four Caesar Salads and New York Strips medium rare... oh, and a couple of bottles of Joseph Phelps Insignia?" he told the waiter. Perusing the room, a few tables had phones perched in the middle, but unless there was a need to call the B.P.L. or B.G.S.D., we would not ask for one.

As the wine flowed, Payton became more and more engaging and, at one point, raising his glass, said, "Boys, shoot low, they're riding Shetlands." Well, no one asked where the line came from, but it was funny! Everyone polished off their perfectly cooked steaks and took a brief respite before departing. On our way out to the sidewalk Payton tripped and fell, almost taking the row of lawn jockeys that guard the entranceway with him. The same gentleman that had made the tie adjustment was there to lend him a hand. "Geez I must have fainted?" said Payton.

Our man at the door wisely joked, " A lot of people do when they get the check in this place."

Sunday morning is the best time to take in the sites of Manhattan. It is generally quiet and you can maneuver around for the most part unimpeded. Once out of The Holland Tunnel it wouldn't take long to reach Route 22 West. The anticipation was building. Was Bill sitting home with *The New York Times* and his cup of coffee wondering to himself whether I really meant to take a look at Watchung before he flew back home? Probably guessed we real estate guys were party animals and wouldn't get up until noon! Wrong!

The Blue Star Highway is a commuter route carved out of hilly terrain. It reminds me a lot of Route 9, a four lane highway that connects Boston to the western suburbs. If a highway like a river has such a thing as a source, then we could say that Route 22 starts in Union Township. We would enter "Commercial Strip" on the working map as the road was dotted with diners, strip shopping centers of all shapes and sizes, and office buildings. There was a Steak and Ale alongside the highway in Mountainside, the only national restaurant that I could see. That was an encouraging sign as the more difficult the entry, the better for us. One downside was that we could not visibly see any residential from the highway, but you could sense that it was there. It was as if Magua in *The Last of the Mohicans* was watching the patrol's every move from the confines of the forest.

They say that beauty is in the eyes of the beholder. The Blue Star Shopping Center was at first blush a site for sore eyes. The Caldor-anchored strip was perched up above the highway, one half of which was blocked from view by a grove of trees. There was a bowling alley, a run of the mill pizza parlor, and another shop that reminded me of Spencer Gifts. There was even a guy selling hot dogs out of truck below grade out by the highway.

Is this a diamond in the rough, I wondered?

The far end of the center was connected to Bonnie Burn Road, and it was on this—call it a "Sunday Drive"—that I knew in an instant that we had a mega-volume opportunity on our hands. Underneath my four wheels was the all important neighborhood access road linking prime residential neighborhoods to Route 22. A Friday's customer could simply drive down the hill avoiding the hassle of Route 22 and park anywhere their hearts desired. But where the hell were we going to put a free standing, 8300 square foot restaurant?

Thinking out loud to myself. 'Caldor is not going to allow us to build in front of their store. There is room down by Bonnie Burn Road, but what about the trees? How about a sign? Where do we put that?' I dialed Bill Harbinger.

"Bill, good morning, No I'm back in Dallas. Got in late Sunday. One hell of a market you have there in Watchung. Of course, took a leisurely drive over on Sunday. My mind was racing with excitement looking for where we could possibly build a Friday's. Let me back up for a second. What about a liquor license?" I waited for his response. "So, you do know that there in one available. Okay, good. And, $175,000 is the range."

Bill and I spoke at length about our options of where the restaurant could go, however, there was only one. Down at the end where the trees were. As for signage, there was a spit of land where the hot dog truck parked where Bill thought a pole sign could go. An individual owned the property, not Heaven Management, and it was in Scotch Plains, not Watchung. Bill knew the guy and thought an equitable arrangement could be made.

Now the hard part. How in the world could I get the site approved? Sherwin? No way. It would be best to start with Buddy. "Bill, the Director of Operations is meeting me in New Jersey next week. The best way from him to see this market will be from the air. When he gets on the ground, well, he may just think that we have gone mad."

Our helicopter was waiting for us at Delaware Aviation at the Northeast Philadelphia Airport. Buddy and I would be able to kill two birds with one stone, or, in better parlance, move forward with these two markets, Princeton and Watchung.

As I was showing the pilot potential landing sites, he quickly dispelled the notion of setting down anywhere in New Jersey. Something about FAA regulations. There were no beer coolers on board, so I figured we'd be okay without stopping.

Buddy noted the helicopter. "Ryan, a Bell Jet Ranger. What gives?"

"I heard they're more reliable," I replied, half jokingly. "Shoe hasn't gotten off my case about Houston by the way."

It wouldn't take but a few minutes to cross over state lines, fly over Trenton, the state capital and reach the Route 1 corridor and Princeton, New Jersey. This Ivy League town with a superior quality of life was, on paper, a real 'sleeper' of a market. Many site selection people in our business were solely into demographics and passed on this market only to scramble for sites and liquor licences once they saw Friday's overwhelming success. When we first took a peek at the number of people in a five mile ring, it was a bit of a shock. Shit, the deer population had to be higher. But wait a second. Wasn't this a classic case of quality over quantity? And let's not forget what was happening in the potato fields of Huntington where farmland was undergoing a rapid transformation to first class office space. The concept of being able to live and work in one community was fast approaching as well.

There was some groundwork to be done in Princeton. Buddy was not into hearing a lot of gibberish, a real joy to be around. He asked for the working map mainly for a navigational aid and set it on his lap. "Buddy," I said, "the market starts where 295 crosses over Route 1. You will see the Quakerbridge Mall on your right. Princeton University is off in the distance to the left." I saw him following along. "Do you see where they are pushing dirt on the west side of Route 1? That's JMB Federated's project called Princeton Marketfair. They want us to saddle up right in front. Friday's will be in line, but we'll be able to have our full trade dress just like a freestander, and our sight lines would be preserved." He nodded in understanding.

Admittedly, the market from the air bore out the demographics. However, Buddy did not ask to look at them, only to say, "Where is everybody, Ryan?"

Confidently, I answered, "They'll be here."

"When we get back," he said, "let's get with the boys and talk about building the smaller prototype that we've been talking about for months. This may be just the market to take it for a test drive."

Roger that! My opinion differed here, however, now was not the time or the place to discuss the matter. That could wait. "Buddy, do me a favor, and run your finger along Route 1 until you get to 287. See it? Now, go west to Route 22."

"Got it. We are on our way to Watchung!"

Buddy reacted much differently as we passed over The Watchung Mountains. There were houses tucked in those hills and lots of them. We could both see the importance of the access road to the neighborhoods; there was no need to even point it out. He glanced at the map, looked out the window, glanced at the map again and as we hovered over the site said, "Ryan, why aren't we down there?"

"We will be, though I must tell you Friday's will not have the best visibility in the world."

Buddy countered, "Can you get me a sign on Route 22? About right where that truck is with the canopy on the side."

"Sure," I said. "We can make that happen."

Friday's had a lease in Princeton sitting on the desk waiting to be signed, but we did not have a handle on a liquor license. The good news was that our location was in the town of West Windsor where there were several active licenses. The bad news was that not every license was for sale and the ones that may have had the best chance to be in play were not being given away. The owners smelled blood when companies like Friday's came a-knocking.

It was time to plan a course of action, so it was off to Princeton to meet with the landlord. There were two terrific companies involved in a joint venture for this project, one of which was a local developer called Carnegie Lake Associates. They had developed the Hyatt Hotel and surrounding office buildings across the street from Princeton Market Fair. It was their Vice President, Roger Buchanan, who made arrangements to meet with me. Buck, as he was called, had narrowed the list down to one operator, a downtrodden Chinese restaurant called the Hot Wok located in a strip center. The owner's name was Russ, and he spoke broken English. Buck monitored the guy's business over the past week, and other than a few take-out orders, there wasn't anybody there. He had to be hurting.

It was decided that I should walk into the Hot Wok that evening unannounced. "Jeff, do you know any Chinese?"

"No, but do you know what 69 is in China?" Buck looked over at me. "Two can chew!"

Buck smiled. "One more please."

"Do you know why there aren't any phone books in China?

"No, why?"

"There are so many Wings and Wongs they are afraid they might wing the wong numba!"

"Very funny, Ryan" Buck scribbled down on a piece of paper: Ni hao. I repeated it, and he told me it meant hello. I wanted to know what we were offering him. "Fire two hundred grand cash at him; he'd be crazy not to accept it." Buck drove me to the location around 8 o'clock.

"Ni hao, I would like to buy your liquor license," I said, "for two hundred thousand dollars, all cash."

Russ returned to check on his soup.

"How about four hundred fifty thousand?" Every counter that I made was answered the same way, with Russ asking for $450,000.

I went back out to the car. "Buck, our guy Russ may not know the English language very well, but he does know his favorite color is green!"

"What did he say?"

"$450,000."

"Are you guys prepared to pay that amount?"

"The amount is pond scum if you look at the big picture. Friday's will be here for two decades or more. Buck, you watch, when the other restaurant companies discover what they are missing out on, they'll be looking for a guy like Russ, or put another way, Russ will be looking for another Jeff Ryan."

"Buck," I said, "I have to place a quick phone call." I dialed up the Boston Public Library. "Yes, I was wondering if you'd be able to tell me how to say $450,000 in Chinese?" As luck would have it, the reference librarian had grown up near Chinatown in Boston and knew some Chinese. She thought she knew how to say $450,000, but she checked anyway. "Yes, Mr. Ryan," she returned to the phone. "It sounds like this: sih yee-by woo-shr yee-chee-ahn." I scribbled it down, and thanked her for her time.

I walked back in and said to Russ, "Ok, Russ, sih yee-by woo-shr yee-chee-ahn."

He stopped stirring. We had a deal.

Buck dropped me off at The Hyatt Regency on Alexander Road. He declined my invitation for a night cap asking for the right to pass because of a school night rule. Thanking him for his efforts, I proceeded to the elevator banks just off the hotel lobby. Making the age old mistake of glancing down at the bar on the lower level, Oscar Wilde was spot on. "*I can resist anything but temptation.*"

Hyatt's signature design element was the atrium, and, if I am not mistaken, the female business traveler had something to do with its evolution. You could walk to your room in plain site of the lobby, avoiding the sometimes dreadful maze of corridors of their competitors. Hyatt listened to the customer. Here the lobby was not quite so dramatic as I recall Buck telling me about a height restriction that they had to confront. So that's why the bar was below grade?

Glancing up from my seat at the bar, I became mesmerized by something as simple as watching the glass elevator stop and start. Simple pleasures for simple minds. In a hypnotic state, I thought about an occurrence that took place in Dallas. The Hyatt had opened a beautiful convention style hotel at Reunion Arena in Dallas, and the setting for their lobby bar was in plain view of three elevators. It was there after a Mavericks game that Baby Cats, Touchdown Tommy and I began wagering on which of the three elevators would reach the top floor ahead of the other two. The money was put on the bar, $20 each, $60 in the pot.

Baby Cats rang in first, "I've got elevator #1."

I picked elevator #2, Touchdown #3, it wasn't long before the folks in our midst caught on to what were doing. A very petite gal wearing a red dress with a figure skater's body came over to ask what all the ruckus was about. "Oh, just wagering on which elevator will reach the top floor first."

"Any chance of getting in?"

"Saddle up with me on elevator #2. Hey guys, let's fatten the bet—I've got another $20 on #2." She grabbed a twenty from her billfold and anxiously watched. It was taking a while; surely someone was staying on the top floor.

"By the way, my name is Rhonda, Rhonda Wilder. Listen, I have an idea," she said, as she raised herself up on her toes to whisper her plan. "Why don't I sneak off to the elevators as if I am going to the ladies room, and if #2 becomes available, I'll jump in and press the button for the top floor."

"Hurry," I whispered. Well she scampered off and, lo and behold, #2 came back down in time for her to make her move. Suddenly, #2 Express took flight for the ceiling. Winner Winner Chicken Dinner!" I collected my—our—winnings.

"Ryan, where'd the girl in the red dress go? She was cute."

"She went to the ladies room; she'll be back," I said with a chuckle. It was time for me to head to the elevators myself.

Watchung proved to be what you can classify as an "impregnable location" and remains that way to this day. No one in the market place has been able to scale the heights and overthrow the King of Blue Star!

THIRTEEN

The Gokstad

Lake Texoma, 90 miles north of Dallas, was built by the Army Corps of Engineers in the 1940s and over the years has become a world class sailing center. The lake's 89,000 acres provides plenty of depth, miles of shoreline and of course ample breezes to fill your sails. Viken Dane honed his sailing skills on this lake. At the beginning, he sailed day-sailers, sloops designed for pleasure and short duration. It was all with one purpose in mind: to someday go deep water sailing, analogous to an amateur turning pro.

In the early 1980s, he took delivery of The Gokstad, a 47 ft. Valiant, a cutter rig built in Seattle and then hauled over land to The Valiant boat yard in the lakeside town of Gordonville for outfitting. The Valiant had plenty of sail power to handle the strenuous conditions of finicky seas and was at the same time a luxurious cruiser. Perhaps it was a fulfillment of a need for adventure or simply his Danish ancestry that led him to this calling. One thing was for sure: he applied the same zealous passion and rigid principles to sailing as he did to his restaurants.

In Limerick, Ireland, there is a barber shop on O'Connell St. owned by Pat Stapleton. His sign on the outside of the door reads: "There is only one God and One Barber: Pat Stapleton is the Barber." [If Pat is still there, stop in and have a shave, the best ever.] Now in Viken's case, there was only one boat and one captain, and Viken was the captain. Interestingly enough, I was the only person to call him skipper, and only around the boat of course. Everyone else called him Viken or Captain Viken, never just captain. Perhaps he reminded me of Kurt Juergens, U-Boat Skipper in The Enemy Below. There was one evening on the boat where, after a few glasses of wine, he did say to me (affectionately of course), "Ryan, you are the most irreverent person I know." Did he say that because I was calling him skipper all day? Maybe.

After her first summer on Lake Texoma, the Gokstad was trucked to Houston for sea trials in The Gulf of Mexico. If the Gokstad had such a thing as a formal crew, Buddy Busch would be the First Officer. Among his many duties, perhaps his most important was assembling a crew. This was to be a hand picked group of volunteers that were looking for adventure on the high seas. Buddy developed a short list and proceeded to conduct interviews in person.

At the very top of the list was Viken's nephew Tiller Dane. Tiller was a management trainee for Friday's, however, he received no special treatment from his Uncle Viken. If anything, he was held to a higher standard than his peers.

Tiller's other talent was that he could play the saxophone like nobody's business. Music played a large role in the boat's ambience. If and when Viken chose to 'go live,' Tiller was called on, Viken would get on the hailer, "Now hear this, now hear this, Musician on Deck.

Buddy did however turn his cheek on one major flaw. (He had to since the pluses outweighed the minuses.) The problem was Tiller's appetite. The boy could eat. A busboy sized tray of deviled eggs at the office Christmas party? He could wipe it out. His favorite dish was probably the Friday's Ultimate Nachos: spicy beef and refried beans under melted cheddar cheese, topped with sliced jalapenos over crisp tortilla chips. The entire plate was his. A three to four day crossing on the Gokstad? There was concern amongst the crew that if the galley did not become off limits at certain times of the day, everyone but Tiller would starve.

Buddy looked at our department for potential candidates. Sherwin was playing tennis competitively, so he was out. Claus was not enthused, only to inform Buddy that Fleet Admiral Chester W. Nimitz was from Fredericksburg, Texas. Bewly was prone to seasickness, so was an automatic scratch. Smoking was prohibited, so that counted Blaze out. Buddy approached me. "You are a golfer, Ryan, so I can't imagine that you'd like to go sailing with us?"

"Hold on Buddy, I'll have you know that my godfather Bill Quinlan is the Commodore of the Ithaca Yacht Club."

"You're in," he said. He put a check mark next to my name. There were several others that made the list. Buddy knew that, just like in our business, there would be casualties. Here you had to be most careful. You can't have someone picked up 600 miles from shore if they don't pan out. Walk the plank or set them adrift were the only options.

The Gokstad had reportedly made its way over to Port Everglades in Ft. Lauderdale and docked at The Marriott Hotel Marina. Viken had set his sights on Great Abaco Island in The Bahamas. On the island's eastern edge a series of cays is renowned for their beauty and easily accessible by private aircraft. Triple Six could pick up the boat's crew and provisions in Ft. Lauderdale and within minutes touchdown at the airstrip in Marsh Harbor. The Gokstad anchored off Man of War Cay, but that was just the start. The open waters of The Atlantic Ocean beckoned to the east.

If memos were a necessary evil, then there was one was one I did not mind reading:

To: The crew of The Gokstad
From: Viken Dane
Subject: Ship's Schedule—Man of War to Hilton Head

Thursday: a.m. Wheels Up-Love Field [Aviall Hangar R]; 10a.m. Arrive Ft. Lauderdale; View Miami site and secure additional supplies. Lunch 1:00p.m.; Depart Ft. Lauderdale 2:00p.m.; Arrive at Marsh Harbor, Abacos 2:30p.m.: Ferry to Man of War Cay; 3:15 Secure provisions-make ready to sail; Cocktails and dinner aboard The Gokstad.

Friday: 5:00a.m. Roll Call; 5:30a.m. Depart Man of War Cay; Breakfast aboard The Gokstad; 7:30 Clear Whale Cay Passage; 8:00a.m. Clear Chub Rock and set course for Savannah, Georgia.

Saturday: Retrieve Booster Rockets for Columbia Space Shuttle.

Sunday: 3p.m. Landfall Hilton Head Island, South Carolina; 5:00p.m. Customs cleared-ship secured; 6:00p.m. Cocktails and Dinner-R&P-Skull Creek Marina.

Monday: 8a.m. Clean Ship and store all gear; 10a.m. R & R -Hilton Head.

Tuesday: 8a.m. Depart Hilton Head; 10a.m. Arrive Love Field-Dallas; Ship's Duties.

Viken Dane, Skipper; Buddy Busch, 1st Officer; Ledger Cockbill, Navigator and Chief Cook; Tiller Dane, Watch Captain; Jeff Ryan, Assistant Watch Captain; Gary Bilger, Sport Fishing; Herbie Hughes Crew Procurer.

Remember: Voter Registration or Passport. One collapsible bag per person. Deck shoes only. Swimsuits, shorts, T-shirts will be prime attire. Hats, suntan lotion, lip balm and a long sleeve shirt are advisable. At least four sleeping bags.

The last attachment to the memo was the all important Watch Schedule. I was particularly excited to see that my partner was Ledger Cockbill. We were to take the third watch on Friday from 2-6p.m. and then a series of watches Saturday Midnight to 3a.m., 10a.m. to 2p.m., and so on.

"Ryan, did you see that we are on watch duty together?" Ledger asked as he peeked into my office holding the memo. Ledger had developed into one of the good guys. He was a natural fit. Restaurant savvy, high standards, enjoyed the good things in life and wanted to win.

"Yes, I was just looking over the crew list. Looks like Herbie Hughes is coming with us."

Ledger, busting chops, nodded his head. "Herbie has had nothing to do for almost a month now." In truth, Herbie was rather busy with all of the store openings. Herbie was in charge of the installation of all of the well-known artifacts on the walls in Friday's. Everything would be shipped by container to the job site, Herbie would then fly in and orchestrate the installation of every single piece to their proper spot on the wall. This was not a haphazard operation. His work was a tedious and time consuming affair. Ledger knew that Herbie would be on the road soon after we returned. There were two openings, a week apart, at the end of July.

"Oh Ledge," I said. "Bewly is picking us up in Ft. Lauderdale. We are going to tour the North Miami market before pressing on."

"Roger that! See you at Hangar R bright and early."

Frito Lay's Canadair was not in the hangar when we boarded Triple Six the next morning, but it got Buddy thinking about the day Flash made the comment. "Wonder where the 601 is today, Ryan?" he said with a smirk. Viken looked back at us with a half-smile and then proceeded to his throne. Technically it was festival seating, with the exception of Viken of course. Buddy was given the nod of sitting opposite Viken, both facing the cockpit. The last person on, which in this case would be Herbie, sat in the jump seat. Once we were airborne he would take on the roll of flight attendant; "Herbie, pass me back a Danish" and "Herbie, get me some coffee."

"How about The Morning News and The Wall Street Journal?" Herbie would ask.

"Don't worry about covering the tray, Tiller is on board remember?"

We settled in for the three hour flight to Ft. Lauderdale. Bewly had briefed me on the North Miami site just in case anyone asked, but he was prepared to answer the questions.

On the plane, I found myself in Bewly's shoes. Before anyone got into the Town Car, he would brief Viken, Buddy and Ledge on the master plan of the Miami-Ft. Lauderdale market. He'd spread the map out on the hood of the car and say, "Gentlemen, here we are in relation to our Friday's at The Falls."

The Falls opened in 1977 at an upscale open-air shopping center, it would be safe to say that if there was ever such a thing as a Friday's Hall of Fame, this store may be the first inductee.

Bewly continued. "The circles on the map represent our targeted markets. This morning, we'll be going here to North Miami where we have locked into a site on Biscayne Boulevard. I though that we could get a much better perspective of the market as it relates to our site if we went on the roof of this high rise condominium. You can see it here on the aerial photograph."

"Not a bad idea," Buddy piped in.

"We should get a move on as the security guard is expecting us. Oh if we have time we can stop at Ernie's for some Conch Chowder."

Bewly conducted the tour with his characteristic polite style. If only they knew the effect darkness bestowed upon Bewly.

Viken, with all his questions seemingly answered, found time for some additional ball busting. As soon as we reached the roof, my acrophobia took over, and I was toast. It was clear to everyone that there was no way I was going anywhere close to the edge. Hugging the walls of the cooling tower, Viken chimed in, "What's the matter Ryan, not feeling well this morning?" He never missed a chance.

After lunch, Bewly bid us bon voyage, and with a fully provisioned aircraft, it was off to Marsh Harbor and the Abacos. Viken pointed out The Gokstad's mooring of Man at War Cay, the daunting Atlantic just off to the east. No one was saying much, but we were all thinking, come morning, that is where we would be, way out there!

The task of provisioning The Gokstad began almost immediately. It was clear from the outset that every item on the boat had its place. You had the sense that even a misplaced toothbrush would be just cause for a reprimand from the skipper. This wasn't a hotel room where you throw down your belongings on the bed and head out the door for dinner.

Viken used the all important cocktail hour to (I say important as this would be our last until landfall in Hilton Head, with the exception of one beer alotted to each crew member when coming off watch duty) emphasize the use of common sense while on board. "Use your lifeline while on duty at night, it would be virtually impossible to find you once overboard. In the rare case that your watchmate ends up in the sea, throw the cushions over the side and then mark your position on the chart. The reason that we keep our lines nice and tidy is so none of us go tripping over them. One last thing, do not be afraid to come and get me if you sense that we are in any danger. Ryan, why don't you go down below and select a coupe of bottles of wine. Ledger is about to announce this evening's menu." Aye, aye, Skipper!

"Gentlemen, tonight we will be having filets stuffed with crabmeat, green salad tossed in tarragon, mixed vegetables and 'barge cake' for dessert. Oh, and don't forget to sign up for the Arrival Pool, $10 each. 1 hour window."

The crew retired early, 5a.m. would come early. Tiller and I grabbed a couple of sleeping bags and slept under the stars. It seemed as if we had just dozed off when we heard music blasting through the Bose speakers surrounding the cockpit.

> *The Eyes of Texas are upon you.*
> *All the live-long day.*
> *The Eyes of Texas are upon you.*
> *You cannot get away.*
> *Do not think you cannot escape them.*
> *From night until early in the morn.*
> *The eyes of Texas are upon you,*
> *til Gabriel blows his horn.*

Out of the corner of my eye, I could see Buddy placing the Texas flag on the stern. They say that sound travels across water; well, everyone on Abaco Island that morning must have thought that they had been taken over by the State of Texas.

After breakfast we weighed anchor and set sail. Past Chubb Rock the aqua color of the water changed. The Gokstad was right at home in deep blue water. Viken standing confidently at the helm gave us one last chance: "If anyone wishes to disembark, now would be the time!" There was a slight moment of silence as if the crew was expected to answer one way or another, but nobody said anything.

Tiller released a flourescent lure from our stern fishing rod. Optimistic that even with our nine knot boat speed, a marlin was sure to strike.

Viken issued the weekend forecast. Temperatures would be in the mid 80s, winds 10-15mph, seas 2-3ft, and sunny skies.

"Now if Tiller could only catch us some dinner. Hell come Saturday evening we could be out of food." Almost instantaneously, the rod bent and we could hear the reel hum. Viken remained at the helm while Tiller made certain that our fish was hooked. Knowing what was coming next, music was needed for the occasion. Before Herbie could find the tape, Tiller launched into "Dinda Dun Da Dunda Da Dunda Dunda Dun Da Da da da." Herbie scrambled for the John Williams CD turning the volume up perhaps so that our Marlin could hear the tune.

Viken had the early time in the Arrival Pool at 13:45 hours, so he was not about to slow The Gokstad for the sake of catching a fish. (Not sure if he knew that I had the latest, four hours later. Somebody had to be last.) Herbie was ready with the gaff and the net.

Generally when a fish sees the stern he will give the old college try and make one last run for it. Not this guy; he was carrying a white flag when he showed up. This poor Marlin was going to be photographed and released. He had some growing up to do!

Music, food, reading, and talking about nothing. From the looks of this crew, you'd never know we were under the immense pressure of a twenty-store opening schedule. Business was left behind for this trip, that was for sure. One thing was for certain; Viken had his pulse on the music. On board were three days of tapes—yes, tapes—created at Midway's world class sound studio. A Music Director's position was created at the office to ensure that the background music in every Friday's was of the highest quality and stayed consistently fresh. All a result of the irascible Viken's visits (unannounced of course) to the restaurants. Upon entering, he would either hear loud and offensive music or no music at all. No longer, Friday's was now going to look after this detail from Midway.

As far as our voyage was concerned, the varietal sounds of

pop, jazz, classical, country western, and show tunes filled the air. Lee Marvin piped in with *Wand'rin Star* from "Paint Your Wagon." Viken, involved in a gin rummy game with Buddy, chimed in without breaking stride. (If only Claus had been there!)

"Wheels are made for rolling, mules are made to pack.
I've never seen a site that that didn't look better lookin back.
Oh I was born under a wand'rin star..."

As evidenced by an entry into the log, the first major glitch occurred sometime during the 12-3a.m. watch. The automatic pilot had malfunctioned, which meant the boat would need to be steered manually. One of the tricks of the trade was maintaining a proper heading with as little deviation as possible. Easier said than done, with a bunch of rookies on board. Ledge and I took over the 2-6p.m. watch that afternoon, and for me this was on the job training as a helmsman.

Viken, experienced as he was, did not have to look at the compass to know that I was having difficulty maintaining our 220 degree heading. He sensed the boat was losing time and distance over the water by the way our sails were acting.

"Ryan, keep your eyes up. You don't drive your car by staring at the dashboard do you?" Guess that was lesson number one, of many. "And you can take that death grip off the wheel as well."

In an attempt to get Viken to focus on something else other than my inability to keep the boat steady. "Ok guys, did you know that the English settlers sailed this very route on their way to Jamestown?"

"That's right, it was all because of the Gulf Stream. Columbus showed everybody the easy way over by riding the ocean current. Once this northbound current was uncovered somewhere in The Caribbean, it made for easy passage northward."

"Geez, Ryan, what have you been staying out of the bars lately?" Buddy cracked.

A MAN SHORT

The diversion had worked as there were no additional reprimands during the remainder of the afternoon. Ledge and I were to relieve Viken and Buddy for the midnight watch so we started preparing early.

It was good to get Viken below. One can easily underestimate the enormous responsibility bestowed upon a boat captain in these situations. Who knows what his level of confidence in us was during the hours he'd be sleeping and entrusting the ship, his precious Gokstad, to our care.

"Ok men, keep your eyes open, we are certain to see a ship or two before dawn," Viken said as he went off to his cabin for the night.

"Ay, ay, skip," Ledge got in a little dig.

It was just past midnight when a blip first appeared on the radar screen. Located on the far outside ring, the object—most likely a ship of some kind, was 16 miles away. It was clear at this point that the watch was no longer a tedious affair. Now we had something to do as it was obvious that whoever was out there was not leaving the screen. Whatever it was, she was heading our way.

"Ledge, it could be a VLCC?" the first thought that popped into my head.

"You may be right; we used to see them come into Long Beach all the time."

"Very Large Crude Carrier: 470 meters in length, 60 ft. at the beam. Shit, they would never even know they hit us."

"Not very maneuverable that's for sure."

We decided to study the directional chart that has four or five different light formations. Green for starboard, red for port and white for steaming. If both masthead lights are in line, you are looking at someone's bow. Unfortunately for us, that was precisely what we saw through the binoculars. The decision was made to roust the Skipper from his sleep.

"Hey Skip," I said after a light tap on the door.

"Yeah, Ryan?"

"I'm afraid we have some company."

"I'll be right there."

Viken was cool as a cucumber as he made his way to the cockpit. Taking a look through the Zeiss binoculars, Viken made an attempt to diffuse the severity of the situation. "Ryan, I could tell that you were at the helm by the way I was rolling from side to side in my bunk." He put the binoculars down and glanced at the radar. "Ryan, go get the crew and tell them to bring their life jackets. We have a VLCC bearing down on us."

Herbie was stunned. "Life jackets? What the hell is the matter?"

"No need to worry. Viken has everything under control. Just one of those big tankers getting a little too close for comfort."

Everyone now on deck, Viken made one last attempt to reach our phantom friend on the radio.

Viken barked the first orders. "Buddy, be prepared to come about. Ledger, hit the strobe light switch. If this bastard doesn't see us, he will now!"

The Valiant's control lines were aft allowing the boat to be easily handled by two able seamen. Viken and Buddy performed the maneuver while the rest of us watched intently. The moonlit sky silhouetted the tanker as we swung away to starboard. Herbie started hollering. "Hey, watch where you are going next time!" he yelled over the water.

"At a boy, Herbie, give 'em hell!" Tiller yelled in support.

Viken returned The Gokstad to 220 degrees and headed below for a visit to the nav station, but not before commenting on how we had done. "Good job fellas." Viken wasn't heavy on the accolades, but if you didn't hear anything to the contrary, you knew you were doing okay.

"Ryan, that shift beer is going to taste mighty good."

"I'll say."

The morning of the Fourth, the music went to 'Patriotic.' Buddy ran Old Glory up the mast to the tune of "You're a grand old flag," the jubilant crew joined in unison.

The anticipation of a Fourth of July celebration started to build with the call of Land Ho! Wait a second, not so fast. "Skipper, could that be our friend from last night?"

"Maybe," said Viken. "She's riding high, that's for sure. Must have discharged her cargo and is hightailing it back for a refill. Let's see if she responds this time. "Exxon Tanker, Exxon Tanker, Exxon Tanker, this is the sailing vessel Gokstad. Come in Exxon Tanker. Over."

After a brief pause we were all delighted to hear a response. "Gokstad, Gokstad, Gokstad, this is the Exxon Tanker Velasquez. Which way you headed? Over."

"Velasquez, we are headed for Hilton Head Island. Over."

"Okay, Gokstad, we will make a right turn and come behind you. Over and out."

The behemoth of a ship passed by us and acknowledged us with one last communiqué. "Gokstad, this is the Velasquez. Enjoy your Fourth! Over."

"Right back at you, Velasquez. Over and out," Viken took the control of the helm as we prepared to enter the estuary where Skull Marina awaited our arrival. "Buddy, would you bring up the chart from below?"

"Right away." But, somehow, Buddy came back empty handed. He came right out with the truth. "I must have left it back at Midway."

Viken remained stoic and ordered us to stand lookout on the bow and yell if we saw any sandbars. Severe currents were churning up the shallow bottom. We had no chance of seeing anything. The Gokstad was on a two mile long crap shoot. Ledge was watching the depth-finder and reporting back to Viken. "Eight feet, cutting close."

The agitated Viken set him straight. "If it's eight feet, then we have a foot and a half clearance until she scrapes bottom." Now inside that, the vitriol reached the bow. "Hey guys, it's not that fucking hard!"

Herbie trying to keep a sense of humor "Fellas, whatever you do, don't fall overboard now—shit—in this current you would catch up with the Valesquez!"

The chart mishap forced Viken's hand. The folks from Skull Creek were going to "talk him in," a humiliating experience, however, he was left little choice. This measure of common sense saved the day. The Gokstad arrived at the dock unscathed.

Tiller retrieved several shot glasses and a bottle of Danish Schnapps from the galley's fridge. A series of toasts took place with the first coming from Herbie. "To Captain Dane—may you die in bed at 95, shot by a jealous wife!"

Next a resounding "here, here," form the crew. With that, Gokstad crew shirts were issued. Viken's invasion plan of Hilton Head called for a two pronged attack, one by land and one by intracoastal waterway. Herbie and Tiller were to take a Town Car to The Quarter Deck, the bar at Harbor Town Marina, and the rest of us were going by Zodiac, a fully provisioned Zodiac at that, as it was quite a lengthy run down the Intracoastal. The white Ashworth crew shirts with The Grokstad prominently displayed on the left sleeve gave the crew a tremendous sense of unity and pride, not to mention a great deal of confidence. The crew assembled in full regalia at the entrance to The Quarter Deck.

Buddy asked to hold on for a moment before we entered The Quarter Deck. "No sense going in there if the ceiling over the bar is too low. Oh, by the way Ryan, before I go in—you'll get a kick out of this—there is a pretty good sized sail boat down there named F U J I M O."

"Fujimo?"

Buddy smirked. "Yeah, it apparently stands for Fuck You Joan, I'm Moving Out!"

Now was the time to showcase Tiller's bar-jumping trick. "Ok, Tiller, it's all yours," he came back out with his thumbs up. Tiller would wait for the right moment before launching. Buddy found some choice real estate at the bar fairly close to the three piece band. A drummer, coronet and sax player fired up Blood Sweat and Tears, gesturing to the crowd to sing along!

"You make me so very happy, I'm so glad you came into myyyyy liiiiife!"

"Ryan, during the break ask these guys if they know Peter Gunn," Viken said. Tiller played this song during his high school band days.

"Excuse me, sir," I said, "is that an alto or tenor sax?"

"Tenor."

"Perfect. Can you guys do Peter Gunn?"

"Sure, of course we can!" they replied.

"You see that handsome devil over there at the bar with the white crew shirt on? The one on the far right," I gestured over there.

"Yeah, what about him?"

"Well, not that it is of any importance to you, his name is Tiller Dane and the man standing next to him is his Uncle Viken. if I can get him to jump on the bar from a standing position, would you mind if he takes a turn on the sax. Sure would make his Uncle proud?"

He thought about it and quickly replied, "Deal." And with that, all that was missing was a drum roll. Buddy grabbed everyone's attention.

"Ladies and Gentlemen! If I may have your attention. My friend Tiller here is going to jump up onto the bar from a standing position. Ok, Tiller, are you ready?" The bartender willingly cleared a spot, and, sure enough, Tiller sprang up like a jack in the box.

The place came apart. Girls flocked to our end of the bar like nobody's business. And then of course the band reciprocateed by summoning Tiller to the stage. He wasted no time strapping on a sax and yelling to the crowd. "Hello, Hilton Head!"

At that moment, a tall and scantilly clad brunette sashayed by the stage. The front of of her shirt read: I AM A VIRGIN! and the back read: THIS IS AN OLD T-SHIRT!

Despite all the fun, it wouldn't be long before Viken would be ready to head back on the Zodiac. Triple Six was scheduled to depart at 8, leaving a short window to clean and secure The Gokstad. Ledge and Buddy would keep him company, Buddy made sure everybody knew the schedule. "Now, boys, you know he'll be pissed if you're not back in time to help clean the boat." We vowed to be there.

Tiller was talking with two very attractive South Carolinians and seemed to be making some headway with his signature ice breaker. "Excuse me ladies, I am from out of town. Can you tell me how I get to your house?"

"My, my, another sailor," they remarked.

"Ladies, allow me to introduce you to the finest helmsman this side of the Atlantic. Meet Commander Ryan."

"Ladies, a Happy Fourth to ya," I said.

"Your friend Tiller here sure has some kind of spring in those legs, and the saxophone!" said one.

"Imagine how he jumps into the sack!" the other remarked.

"He'll make one hell of a wave on my water bed! I wouldn't be able to stay on board!" she giggled. "By the way, my name is Tilly and this is my friend Lilly. Where you Yanks from anyway?"

"Dallas. Tilly, Lilly, how about if we do some shots?" I suggested.

"We thought you'd never ask."

"Name your poison. Tequila, kamikazes?"

"Commander," she said, "goodness how boring! Slippery Nipples! Innkeeper, four Slippery Nipples."

"Coming right up."

"Where'd the rest of the crew go? Past their beddy bed time?"

"Yes, we've got an early start tomorrow," said Tiller. "The plane leaves at 8 and the skipper lives by the motto 'A clean boat is a happy boat,' so he'll be up at the crack of dawn."

The girls noticed the Gokstad logos on our shirts. "Where is she docked?"

"Skull Creek Marina."

"Well I guess you better get a move on, sailors, that's way up north of here."

"No," we assured them, "we don't have to be home till 6."

The girls seemed pleased at this. "Well, then, what do you say we party with a couple of Yanks? Jeff, sugar, let's do some more shots. Sex on the Beach, how about it?"

"Can we?" I asked, very much interested in this Lilly.

"Of course we can. Innkeeper, more shots."

The girls had some idea of where they wanted this night to head. "Boys, it's gettin' near the bewitchin' hour."

"Well how about if we take you Yanks to a Confederate Bar across the river. "We can make it there by last call."

"The only time I say no," said Tiller, "is when a girl has asked me if I have had enough!"

The four of us piled into the front seat of Lilly's perfectly worn Chevy pick up, slight tears in the upholstery, faded dash, cracked paint on the hood.

"What, no music?" Tiller asked.

"My ex busted the radio," Lilly replied.

"What a dumbass for lettin' you go," I said softly. The truck pulled into a place called Savannah Danna Doos. "Boys, if we hurry, we can have one more shot just before they play Dixie.

Don't worry, they accept Yanks in here."

Lilly knew the bartender "How about four red headed sluts, JW?"

"Coming right up, Lilly."

"We didn't miss Dixie, did we?"

"Next song," JW replied.

Despite all the whiskey, it gave me chills to hear everyone come together for Dixie.

> *"Oh, I wish I was in the land of cotton,*
> *Old times there are not forgotten,*
> *Look away, look away, look away Dixie Land."*

"Come on," Lilly said shortly after the first verse. "Let's smuggle the Yanks out of here. Just to be safe. "Come on guys, let's go to our place. It's just down the road a piece." Lilly took us down the dirt road to a ramshackle house hidden behind a Southern Magnolia tree. As soon as we pulled in, we could hear the dog. I asked if he was friendly, Lilly replied "that's Major, my German Shepherd. He's pretty protective."

"The ex kick him too?" I asked.

She laughed. "The ex was scared shitless of the dog."

It just occured to me, how on earth are we going to be able to make any romantic moves with a guard dog that apparently hates guys watching our every move. "Let's sit out on the porch," Lilly suggested, "I'll grab some cold ones."

Tiller and I knew we'd gotten ourselves into a real doozy of a mess. Here we were, in the middle of God knows where and the girls were getting sloppy drunk.

"Commander, I think I'm going to be sick," she said, running back inside.

Excellent, just excellent, I thought. We've got one about to be doing the commode hug and another ready to pass out. "Tiller, I didn't realize women snored. Aren't we the only ones allowed to do that?"

"Ryan, it's 4:30 and we're on some dirt road in Savannah. The Skipper starts his scrub-a-dub-dubbing in an hour and a half!" More aware of our predicament by the second. "Now what do we do?"

"Keep Major occupied while I call a cab."

"A cab?"

"Any other suggestions?"

"Okay, a cab."

Slowly, I made my way back to the kitchen, realizing there was no way I'd be able to find a phone book. The clock on the stove read 4:55. My pulse quickened. I spotted a pink wall phone and dialed information.

"What city and state?"

"Savannah, Georgia."

"One moment please." Information connected me to the Yellow Cab number.

"Hello! Yellow Cab!"

"Listen, we're a couple of stranded Yanks over by Savannah Danna Doos trying to get back in a hurry to Skull Creek Marina."

"What's your address."

"Uhh," I stalled, searching around the junk on the tabletops for something with an address on it. Shit, not even a phone bill. I was getting impatient. "You know where Savannah Danna Doos is? We are near there, there is a house with a big magnolia tree out front."

The dispatcher chimed in "Boy, you think there is only one magnolia tree in Savannah, you ah sawly mistaken! You think it's funny wastin' my time like this, don't ya?"

"I'm sorry, sir, I just don't know the address. We're near Savanna Danna Doos, magnolia tree, uh, uh, there's a nasty German Shepherd!"

"Oh, you mean Major?" his tone changing. "Well, I'll be damned, you horny yanks are at Lilly's place. You boys better hope JW, the new boyfriend, doesn't swing by and check in on her."

"He's not the ex?" I asked timidly.

"No, JW's not the ex," he chuckled. "Shit, the bartender is her boyfriend."

"Listen," I pleaded, "can you get someone over here pronto? We've got to get to Skull Creek Marina or our ass is grass." I suddenly missed my favorite cab driver from back in Dallas.

"It'll be $100 to Skull Creek."

"Listen, there's $50 extra in it for you if we get to the boat by six." It seems this was a standard practice of mine, giving taxi drivers extra money to meet my scheduling needs.

"You boys meet me down the end of the street. But be careful not to piss Major off."

"How do we do that?"

"Slowly walk backwards out of the front yard then turn around and run for the truck. Major will give chase, but only for 50 yards or so."

"Tiller, here's the deal. Our ride is on the way. Let's slowly walk backwards until we get halfway down the street, and then take off." By the time we inched our way down the dirt road, our cab was waiting for us.

"Tiller, on the count of three. One... Two... See ya, Major!" The driver was right; the dog came to a screeching halt at the end of the road. It was close, but we made it.

The sun was coming up as we crossed back over the bridge. Viken and the rest of the crew were hard at work by now. Tiller and I looked at each other like two condemned men ready to face the firing squad.

"Buddy," Viken said, "looks like I win!"

"No one had you two coming back this early!" Buddy said, referring to the pool they had going on us.

Viken, not losing a chance to get in a good dig, perked up. "Oh yeah," he said, smiling up at us from his position on deck. "We saved the heads for you guys! Get 'em nice and clean!" They all laughed. "What do you guys say? Should we go get some breakfast while these two finish up?"

And so, our last morning on the Gokstad was spent scrubbing toilets and recovering from the events of the night before. It was safe to say we were ready to return to Dallas.

FOURTEEN

Boston

It wasn't long before Triple Six reached its assigned altitude and left Hilton Head behind. It was Monday morning, and the game was back on. We used the flight to gather some of our thoughts.

Ledge was looking over the Development Schedule, about which there would be questions. We, of course, always had in the back of our minds what was happening within our respective territories first, and then the national scene second. At that time, we were viewing the Northeast Corridor a certain way as I recall. Princeton to the south was at the foot of "the bed." Albany was at the head, a big fluffy pillow. Underneath the covers were Watchung, Eatontown, Woodbrige, Westbury, Huntington, Tarrytown, Albany, and on up to Warwick. Pretty good bedfellows. Before the blankets could be pulled all the way up, to continue the analogy, there were Hartford, Norwell and Danvers, Mass. in the way, and they needed to be put to bed. Those markets had always been on the agenda.

Ledge got after it. "Ryan, if you add Philadelphia to the mix, which is Blaze's territory, correct?"

"That's right."

"And we look at Albany and everything in between," said Buddy.

"Then Friday's," Ledge continued, "will be operating a $50,000,000 dollar business in the Northeast in another two years. I see Norwell is the first to open in 85." He paused. "Ryan, your Albany site was the first in 84; that may be a good sign."

I was more confident than that. "It will be a sensational hit," I said.

"Why's that?" they asked.

"There is huge pent-up demand for restaurants in Suburban Boston," I explained. "For years, everybody, including me, traveled into the city. Now it's time to bring the city to the suburbs." As it turned out, this wasn't going to be an easy accomplishment, the people we needed to win over (Board of Selectmen) didn't exactly want the city infiltrating their peaceful suburbs. One of the most significant obstacles we faced was overcoming the reputation of Friday's as being a singles bar, a reputation that was solidified in the minds of those residing outside the city and which wouldn't be easily overcome. We had to find a way for them to accept the idea of having a Friday's in their community.

Ledge continued with his plans. "There are architectural issues with the town of Norwell that need to be addressed. They are into Colonial style buildings, which hasn't really been done so far for a Friday's, but there is room for compromise along the way."

Buddy said "If colonial architecture is what gets these people to accept us out in the suburbs, we'll sure have to entertain that idea."

Ledge continued, "Ryan, you are planning as it stands now to show Clavin and Sherwin the market from the air?"

"The realtor that brought us the site is a pilot, actually. Single fan piper cub."

"Be like one of those scout planes that Henry Fonda flew in The Battle of The Bulge," added Buddy.

"Indeed. We'll take it down to treetop level just to give them a better view."

Viken was lost in thought. Despite Ledge's optimism, the

onslaught of openings weighed heavily on his mind. The numbers that were coming back were telling us that the new stores needed more time to gain momentum. There was no turning back though, as we were at the mid-point in July.

"San Mateo opens in August," Ledge said. "You been out there, Ryan?"

Oh yeah, have I ever, I was thinking to myself. "Yeah I have," I said. "That's Claus's deal. It will be a good one."

"How is Claus by the way? Since the divorce I mean," Ledge asked.

"He's out there playing the field. Had a new gal for a while that seemed to be going okay until the card arrived," I explained.

"What card?"

"Oh you didn't see it?" I said. I thought the whole office knew. "He showed it to us the other day. Just a plain white card with bold black letters on the front, which read: I CAN SEE INTO THE FUTURE. The message continued on the inside of the card with: AND YOU'RE NOT IN IT. It was signed "So Sorry, Susan."

"How brutal," said Ledge. "Did you ever meet her?"

"Oh sure," I said. "Nice girl from Atlanta." That got a chuckle out of everyone; even Viken was amused.

"Let's find out what card shop that came from," said Ledge. "Shit, I could use plenty of those!"

There wasn't much time to unpack as the trip on Wednesday up to Boston was coming. This trip would involve an entourage: including a new architect that was going to bring some renderings of the Norwell exterior. Blaze was going to tag along as well and then drive Clavin and Sherwin down to Westchester County. He was at his desk when we walked in on Monday.

"Ryan, nice shirt," he said taking in the Gokstad logo. "What are those, stains on the front?"

I looked down, unsure of what he meant and then noticed the

spots myself. "Shit, I didn't realize it. Jello shots, Sex on the Beach shots, you name it.... Pretty crazy evening last night." I started to tell him the story, but decided to save it for the ride up to Boston.

Tuesday, there was a personal matter to attend to. A trip to Rosemeade Veteninary Clinic in Carrollton confirmed that Colonel's cancer had indeed spread to his nose, making it difficult for him to breath. The veterinarian thought that I should sign a euthanasia agreement just in case. Admittedly, I had a very tough time holding my emotions in check as we both waited for the paperwork. Once in the car, Colonel reassured me that everthing would be OK by customarily resting his head on my shoulder from his position in the back seat. Reaching my right hand up and over his right ear, his tail wagged as I scratched a hard to reach spot. Irish Setters have a renowned childlike behavior and Colonel was not about to let go of that trait no matter how dire the circumstance.

Hank, his handler at Toothacres, had become very close to Colonel and assured me that he would look in after him while I was in Boston. The kennel was situated on a former cattle ranch. There was plenty of room to walk the canine guests and let them run around. I left Betty's number with him, and he promised to call her if anything happened.

The five of us met Wednesday morning at 7a.m. at the American Airlines gate for the flight to Boston. It was my first trip with this new architect, Fred Lollypop. I confess I didn't know what to make of him after I heard him say to another passenger, "I don't know why we are flying out so early; there's a flight this afternoon that would get us in at five."

Clavin and I sat next to each other. Clavin was much better after the dumpster incident. His grandstanding days were over with this group.

"Ryan," he said, "I guess we're sort of taking you back home this morning."

"Yeah," I said, "it'll be good to show you guys the old stomping ground."

"Sherwin was telling me the Norwell developer is having financial difficulties?" he asked.

"Yes, we have a back up plan fortunately," I told him. "The Warwick developer is likely coming to our rescue and will do the deal."

"Fantastic."

"You will see the Norwell site from the air tomorrow morning actually. Today we we're going to take a drive up to the North Shore to look at our Danvers site. We are working with a terrific developer, the Gutierrez Company."

"Where are we staying?"

"Braintree, just a little outside Boston. Tomorrow we'll have a full day on the South Shore. We'll see the site from the air first, like I said, and then we'll see it on the ground too. After that, Blaze will drive you down to Westchester County."

"Sounds like a plan, Ryan. Can't wait to see what you've got for us."

"Should be good, Clavin," I said. "Ever been to Beantown before?"

"Never."

"Well, just remember to fasten your seatbelt; driving is a competitive sport up here," I told him.

We landed at Logan and picked up the rental car. From there, we headed over the Tobin Bridge. My man Lollypop was wondering when we were going to stop for lunch. Boy was he in for a surprise. This was a real estate car, and day time was for work, not lunch.

After we'd set off for a little bit, Sherwin began nodding off. Not Blaze, though, he had his ears pinned like a Doberman, always curious and ever alert to the goings on. "Ryan," Blaze said, "what's up with these restaurants the size of aircraft carriers?

The Hilltop Steakhouse, my word. The plastic cow or whatever that thing is over there is bigger than a house!"

"You know Blaze," I said, "I have never been in to eat there."

"What the hell does this strip look like on a Saturday night?" asked Blaze.

"Four lanes of hell, that's what. Friday's will be much better off where it is a bit more civil. We will just stay on this road and we will run right into a good spot, I promise you, Blaze."

Soon, we made it to Danvers and I pulled into the site. "Ok boys, time to wake up," I said, looking in the rearview mirror at Sherwin. "We're home. Here is or our pad site next to the Hard Cover."

Sherwin looked around. "Shit, Ryan, this could be the first restaurant park in The Northeast," said Sherwin.

"That's what I said." Evidently, Sherwin was catching on. "They are going to reserve it for an office building, so we'll see. Anyway, fellas, this is pretty straightforward stuff," I said, giving them the rundown. "Route 114 dissects the market, so we really are at an intersection of Route 1 and Route 114. It doesn't have the appearance of that, but that is where we win big time. All the retail shopping is carried out right out there, and it gets messy. Traffic backs up like in Dallas. Here, we have more range of motion."

"I see what you're saying," said Clavin. "The parking field is plenty big enough. Is that a big office building up on the hill?"

I laughed. "No, man, it's a nut house actually. Every good market has one!" My next plan was something I often did to give newcomers a sense of their bearings in an unfamiliar location. "Let's drive three or four miles in each direction," I said, heading back toward the car. "That should give you a good feel for what is going on."

"Ryan," said Sherwin, "we may have to feed Fred before he passes out."

"Well, we don't usually stop for lunch, but if you insist. Romie's Oyster House, we'll go there."

Sherwin, once again out of the clear blue, reverted back to being a real estate jockey. He found a moment alone with Blaze and me. "Fellas, after dinner, let's tuck these gizz balls in bed and go on back out. What do you say?"

"Sounds like a plan," I said. "Boston is only 12 miles from the hotel. Shit, We'll go to the Black Rose, a great Irish Pub over by Faneuil Hall."

After lunch, we resumed our market tour taking the coast road south from Marblehead, Swampscott and Revere. At least Paul Revere rode alone; this was becoming torture. After riding around a bit, we decided to make it into the city and visit the Newbury Street location.

Clavin commented on my driving, "Ryan, you sure know your way around. I take it these are little short cuts?"

"Yeah, I know the streets pretty well. You have to with all the congestion. I drove an inter-company mail truck one summer for The New England Telephone Company visiting all of their branch offices in a Ford Econo-line Van. This was during a long protracted strike so they had a member of management drive around with us. Made you drive a lot faster."

Successfully parked, Sherwin led the charge inside. Before entering, he made sure to turn and remind us that we were about to enter the #1 singles bar in Boston. At the time, that news was all over The Boston Globe. It was on our radar as well, and we were well aware of the problems the press coverage presented for our store openings.

We bypassed the bar, which was jamming at three deep, and went straight to a table. Sherwin ordered a bottle of the B/V Beau Tour and two appetizers: zucchini slices coated with a seasonal batter, deep fried and served with Parmesan cheese ($2.25), and Friday's onion rings, cut large, breaded with buttermilk batter and fried golden, an item served with a shaker of Parmesan cheese when requested ($1.95). Blaze, of course, stuck with his standard glass of Chivas.

For me it was time to hit the head. Stepping up to the urinal, I noticed two pairs of shoes in one of the stalls. That's interesting, I thought. Then I heard a small bit of conversation. This guy's got a dollie corralled inside there. My hero! It seemed, however, that she had second thoughts. Meanwhile, he was backpedaling, saying, "Oh you have to be emotionally involved right?" This guy had all the lines.

"Boys," I said, returning to the table, "You missed it. Some guy's in there making an attempt at joining the restaurant version of the mile high club by cornering this gal in the men's room stall. Don't think he closed the deal. Got to give him an A for effort though."

After dinner, we jumped on The Southeast Expressway and in no time were at The Sheraton Tara in Braintree. Sherwin gave us the signal behind Clavin's back to meet back in the lobby in 15 minutes. The plan for the next morning was set: everyone was to assemble downstairs for coffee at 7a.m.

Sherwin, Blaze, and I then headed back into the city. The Black Rose had great live music and we knew it would be busy. A table opened up by the stage just as we walked in, so we grabbed it quickly. Blaze ordered his Chivas, Sherwin his Dewars and water, and for me a pint of Guinness. Glancing around the room, we saw two gals sitting by themselves.

"Ryan," Blaze said, "go fetch! The night isn't getting any younger."

The girls were at a nearby table. "Ladies, you are looking lovely this evening! We'd be honored to have you join us at our table." I pointed to a smiling Sherwin and Blaze. They said they'd think about it—it sounded like a yes to me, so I snatched their purses off the back of the chairs. I returned to our table,

A MAN SHORT

plopping the newfound bounty in front of the guys. "The girls will be here in a minute."

The girls came over, sure enough. Sitting next to me was Maggie Kelly. "Nice move with the purses, do you get away with that often?"

Blaze and Sherwin soon realized that Maggie's friend was not into socializing so the table turned their attention to the stage. An Irish band was just about to start the final set of the evening. Maggie pulled her chair closer to mine much to the chagrin of my running mates. Sherwin ordered a couple of rounds of Bushmills for last call. Now Mr. Smarty pants with nothing to lose asks Maggie's friend if she had any Irish in her?

Her response was a curt no, in which Sherwin replied "would you like some?" with that she was off to the parking lot. Maggie and I were headed to Malden, so we directed Blaze and Sherwin to the Southeast Expressway. See you bright and early boys!

Malden is considered inner city so it was a short ride to her place. "Maggie," I said, "can we make sure we get up early enough so we can beat the morning traffic through the city?"

"Yeah, don't worry; both my roomate and I are early risers."

Once inside her apartment, Maggie wasted no time as we by passed her roomate's bedroom and jumped into the sack. Foreplay was not on her agenda. After all her digital clock showed 1:45a.m., there wasn't much time—or perhaps she noticed the Bushmills taking hold on me. She did broach an interesting question to me in the heat of passion. "Jeff, before the night is over would you mind inserting your projectile in my ass?" I can't quite recall how I may have responded. However, that wasn't the thought inside the bubble over my head. *Why take the dirt road when the highway is available!*

The adventure began at 6a.m. the next day, early, though certainly not enough time to be in the hotel lobby at 7a.m. I was able to think ahead and call the front desk of the hotel prior to leaving Maggie's apartment. I told the receptionist to please call up to the others to let them know I'd be about 15 minutes late. Maggie understood the severity of the situation and sprang into action. If the guys were impressed with my driving the day before, they'd have been much more impressed with her navigation from Malden to the hotel. We made it to the front door of the Sheraton Tara at 7:20; not bad.

Standing in the doorway were Clavin and Lollypop. Maggie wrote her number down, and we gave it the old one night stand smooch. The automatic doors opened. "Morning, guys," I said, "looks like we have a nice day for a plane ride." Looking at their expressions, I said, "The front desk did call right?" They weren't happy, I could tell.

"You may want to see what Sherwin and Blaze are up to," Clavin said.

I couldn't believe they still weren't up. I ran up to the front desk. "Excuse me, would you please call Mr. Bliss and Mr. Bomberkoff's room?" The front desk clerk dialed as I rushed into the elevator. Sherwin cracked his door open as I walked by, and I could see he had nothing but his BVDs on. "Ryan," he giggled, "we are digging our own grave." With that, he shut the door.

My being twenty minutes late paled in comparison to this problem. Sherwin and Blaze were still tanked from the night before. They finally came fumbling down with their luggage. Looked like it was going to be a long day for this foursome. There wasn't a great deal of conversation that morning. The car smelled like a scotch bottle. Can't imagine what the tiny compartment of the plane would smell like. It was hard to know what was going through Fred's mind, since he was new. Blaze would keep him straight while we took to the air.

Dick Leahy, was patiently waiting for us at the Norwood-Airport. "Fellas, allow me to introduce you to Dick Leahy, Realtor Pilot Extraordinaire, Oh-Great-One of The South Shore.

"Jeff, who is coming with us?" he asked.

"Sherwin and Clavin. Dick, let's put Clavin in the right seat. Sherwin and I will get in the back."

"Time to take a nap," said Sherwin.

Leahy had been out with us before. "At The Black Rose again?" he asked.

"Yup! Can't seem to stay away," I said. "Here, Clavin, spread the map out on your lap. Dick, will you fly over to this point where you see "Mall?" That is The South Shore Plaza owned by Corporate Property Investors. This point is the beginning of The South Shore. Emphatically, there isn't any room for us there, or for anybody else for that matter."

"Is that the 100%?" Clavin asked.

"Yes. We are comfortable drifting down 8 miles," I said, demonstrating by running my finger down the map. "Norwell is in the heart of the residential market. Keep in mind, Clavin, this isn't Texas where you can build anywhere you like."

Leahy added, "Okay, guys, we are directly above the Barnside in Hanover?"

We wrote that in big letters. "That is a mega volume restaurant next to Norwell. The guy that owns it does not want to see a Friday's down the street. He'll fight us tooth and nail, but we feel we can win the two out of three votes needed to get our license."

"If you say so, boss," said Clavin.

Sherwin started to nod off. This may be a godsend, as his breath reeked of scotch and cigarettes. A tell tale sign that Sherwin had gone over the edge was when he fired up a burner. At the Black Rose he was matching Blaze butt for butt. Sherwin, drifting in and out of his coma, was making funny faces in the direction of the cockpit. I shushed him, but it didn't work. "Go back to sleep, will ya?" mouthing my words.

Dick banked the scout plane over I-95. Clavin got a bird's eye view of all the homes that otherwise would be nearly impossible to see from the ground. Next, Dick swung out over the site and headed east towards the oceanside towns of Hingham and Cohasset. "Look, guys," Dick said, "those are all of your customers down there waiting for a good restaurant."

The hard landing woke Sherwin up. Dick just smiled; he himself had been in Sherwin's position at least once or twice.

"How did it go, fellas?" Blaze greeted us.

Sherwin, stumbling off the ramp, replied, "Well, any landing you walk away from is a good one."

"Mr. Leahy," Fred said, "here are the renderings of the exterior that you asked for. There are some Colonial features that we added to our prototype as you requested. We thought you would enjoy the changes." That Fred sure did try hard.

"Great, Fred," Dick replied. "And, please, just call me Dick."

Blaze wanted to make a pit stop. "Ryan, let's do a cursory swing by the site but stop for some coffee first. These boys need to sample some of the high test that all these people are hooked on up here. What is it that we ask for? Reg-u-lah?"

"Yes," I said, "that's with cream and sugar. You should know they are not shy with the sugar."

"You know, Fred doesn't know whether to believe you or not. Where's The Clam Box you keep raving about, Ryan?"

He made a good point. I definitely had meant to take them there. After ordering our coffees and getting rid of the "shakes," we continued. From Norwell, we drove past the Barnside out to the coastal road 3A and slowly worked our way to Logan. Fred became quite the inquisitive tourist, and I suppose I stepped into the role of enlightening tour guide.

"Jeff, is that a shipyard up ahead?"

"Fore River Shipyard actually. Pretty busy place during WWII. They pumped out Spruance Class destroyers, even the keel of the battleship Massachusetts." As we drove over the Fore River Bridge, Blaze came alive. "Ryan, anybody you know jump off this bridge?"

"Just one, my Uncle Mert. He rode the current to the shore over by the Proctor and Gamble soap factory. What a pisser... a bona fide adventurer." Blaze saw an opening.

"So not everyone in your family is acrophobic."

"Anyway, my father and his three brothers all worked there from one time or another. The youngest, Ralph, is now a big time executive in the industry. One of the brothers, James, came home one day to report to my grandmother Helen that he had lost his St. Christopher medal somewhere on The Massachusetts. She in turn replied, 'Well, it sure in hell won't sink now, will it?' She was right! The ship is now moored safely at Battleship Cove in Fall River."

"What's James up to now?" asked Blaze.

"James went on and volunteered for the 10th Mountain Division and was killed in action in the Italian Campaign less than a month before the war ended. Actually, we're going to come up on the Mt. Hope Cemetery just about now. James is laid to rest there next to another brother, Richard, a ball turret gunner on a B-24 Liberator called The Club 400."

"Quite a lineage, Ryan," Clavin said.

"Sure is. Richard flew out of a base in San Giovanni, Italy. They crossed over the Alps to hit targets like the Ploesti oil fields in Romania."

Fred piped up. "I have a question. How would you know the name of the plane? You say it was called the Club 400."

"Well," I explained, "Liberators were manufactured at two plants in the states. One in Willowbend outside of Detroit and the other in Ft. Worth. The *Dallas Sunday Morning News* ran an article on the 50th anniversary of the first Liberator that rolled off the assembly line. Shit, I got in the car and raced over there with my Uncle's Bomb Group and squadron number that I took off the grave stone. If I remember right, it was the 485th

Bomb Group, 736 Squadron. Anyway, I was hoping to run into a member."

"How did you make out? Any luck?" Blaze asked. By this time, we were on Quincy Shore Drive and Wollastan Beach.

"Yeah, I did end up getting lucky, but not that day. An Army Air Force vet told me to put an ad in the San Giovanni Times, a newsletter that was circulated amongst the surviving crew members. So, I did."

"What'd it say?" asked Clavin.

"Something like: Nephew of Sgt. Richard Ryan, killed in action, April 13, 1944, looking for information, and so on. Never did I think that anyone would respond when lo and behold, one Sunday afternoon, a gentleman introducing himself as Clemm called to say that he was the waste gunner on board that fateful day. My heart dropped to say the least. 'Well, Jeff,' he says, 'There is good news and bad news here. I am not sure what you would like to hear first, so I'll tell it altogether. We were headed for The Tokol Aerodrome outside of Budapest. After a successful bomb run, the formation of 300 planes was to turn right and head for home. The Club 400, piloted by a rookie, turned left leaving us isolated. Me 109s were all over us. One came up from underneath the aircraft, and, well, it got your uncle. You know, Jeff, the early 24's didn't have the ball turret, but when the belly of the aircraft became exposed to this maneuver, the ball turret was installed. Our plane managed to get away, but not before taking a great deal of fire. If there is any consolation, we shot down the 109. 'Clemm, one last thing. The Club 400?' It was a great saloon in New York City that a bunch of them had been to on numerous occasions."

By now, we'd arrived at The Clam Box. "Come on, boys, let's get some clams!" We grabbed a picnic table and ordered. Clavin had by now come around after this morning's debacle. "Good trip so far," he said. "Ryan, we'll drop you off at Logan and head for New York."

I looked at my watch. "Tell you what guys, let's get going, that way you guys can dodge the southbound traffic coming out of Boston. Take the clams with you; it will drown out the smell of scotch on Sherwin's trench coat! Plus, there is an important call I need to make from The Admirals Club."

There were memories that crept back into my head on this ride. I kept the thoughts to myself and let my passengers carry on their own conversation; I nodded from time to time or gave it the cursory 'yeah, I remember that.' In plain view was the house at 14 Hummock Road where my father grew up. On this day, I was specifically thinking of my father's mother, Helen. She demonstrated unrelenting faith after the devastating loss of her two sons. All the while not knowing the fate of my father who remained on convoy duty in The North Atlantic.

My thoughts were temporarily interrupted by Blaze. "Never seen you this quiet, Ryan," he may have thought it was about Colonel, so he backed off.

In the summer of 1981, Helen passed away, having outlived her Irish born husband by some 27 years. This was the first and only time that I saw my father cry. After the ceremony he began to rush up the hill to visit with his fallen brothers, his sister, my Aunt Dottie, yelling to him "Don't go there, Bob, don't go there!" In the car, my emotions almost got the best of me thinking of that touching scene.

It was ironic that we then entered The Callahan Tunnel and just a few minutes away from Logan. "Ryan," Fred, my able tourist asked, "Who is this Lt. William Callahan?"

"Well," I said, "if I can slow down without getting yelled at, you will notice that underneath his name it reads '10th Mountain Division 85th Infantry Company F.'"

"By golly, it does. Next you are going to tell me that Lt. Callahan and your Uncle James fought alongside each other."

"Right you are, Fred. They were in fact in the same outfit and perished only days apart."

We reached curbside at American, and we all shook hands.

"See you guys back at the ranch!" I said. "Blaze, take care of these guys!" There was plenty of time to take care of an upgrade at The Admirals Club and hopefully say hello to Tale Wind at the gate. I figured it was also a good time to check in with Betty. There was a spot in the corner of the Admirals Club where there was some peace and quiet and a phone. I dialed her up. "Betty, how are things?"

"Hey, Ryan, you taking good care of my Sherwin?"

"It's not easy, but yes I am. Blaze has got the baton now! Should be off to New York by now. Any calls for me?"

"Oh, yes, a bunch, but before I give them to you. Toothacres called."

"Did they say what they wanted?"

"No, just that you should call."

"Okay. Hold the other messages Betty until I get back. Thanks, see you soon."

Hank picked up the phone. "Jeff, I'm glad you called. Listen, I went to walk Colonel this morning, and he wasn't moving. I'm so sorry. He must have died in his sleep, bless the Lord." Having delivered the news, Hank was sobbing.

"Don't cry, Hank, you'll get me going," barely holding it together. "Hank, let's have him cremated and make up a stone for him. Pick out a good spot for him in The Garden of Memories?"

"Yes of course, we'll take care of that right away. Mr. Ryan, he was just a great dog, that Colonel."

Before my voice let go, I said goodbye and slumped in my chair. It was probably a good thing that it was boarding time as my mind had to think about getting on the plane. There would be plenty of time to ponder Colonel soon enough.

"Hi, Tale, how is everything? You're looking good."

"Hey, Mr. Ryan. Can't get enough of Boston I see. What is it, the girls are better looking up here?"

"No question! Always one to look out for me, I see that you are dining in the sky this evening."

"See ya pal!"

It was nice to sit by the window for a change; this way no one could bother me on the way back. My emotions were running in every different direction, although it wouldn't be until we got home that the reality of the situation would hit me. The plane ride offered me a welcome chance to just simply stare into the clouds and reflect on my four legged companion of 13 years. Colonel Cornelius O'Ryan was his official AKC name.

Growing up, boxers were our breed of choice the first being Sparkle, who would sit patiently beside my mother on the front steps of our house until such time as my sister, brother and I returned from elementary school. He must have had a built-in clock to know when we would first appear. Once in sight, he would leave my mother's side and race up to the top of the hill to escort us home.

There was our long haired Dachshund, Schultz, who when seeing my brother Rich pack for college would lay in the driveway in back of the car. I am sure he would have sacrificed himself if we didn't pick him up. Last but not least, there was Kelly, my sister's Salt and Pepper Schnauzer. For some reason unbeknownst to me, he slept at the foot of her bed under the covers. I always wondered how he did that night after night; did he have a secret air hole?

Schultz, more business-like, would lead his two mischievous house guests on his traditional hunt for woodchucks in the nearby woods. It always struck me as funny that the three would depart at the same time, but never return together. One thing was for certain; they came back home looking like Sherwin and Blaze must have the night I left them for Maggie's house: a mess.

The fight attendant must have caught me smiling out the window as I thought of these memories. "Excuse me, sir? Can I get you anything?"

Startled out of my daydream. "Oh, wonderful, sure, let's see. Scotch."

"We have The Glenlivet on board. Will that be okay?"

"That will be more than okay. Thank you so much." I stretched out my legs, reclined my chair, and gazed out at the sky, illuminated with the bright tones of sunset. In my thoughts, I toasted Colonel and the time we'd spent together. 'Colonel, I'll miss you.'

FIFTEEN

The Final Charge

At long last, 1984 was coming to a close. There were several critical planning and zoning meetings to attend, each one having its own nuances. Eatontown, New Jersey, for example, would put you on their agenda, but would not necessarily get to us on that particular evening. I suppose they thought they were getting off the hook by warning us in advance that this might happen. The attorney would say to us after looking at the evening's agenda, "This doesn't look good; there is a good chance that we will have to come back next month." Despite the dysfunctional nature of this system and others like it, we remained patient.

In Norwell, there was stiff opposition building, reportedly fueled by our friend at The Barnside. Every citizen that showed up at one of these hearings was entitled to due process. The more citizens Mr. Barnside sent in, the more hearings it would take to diffuse the situation. An independent restauranteur may have caved in, but when word filtered back to Midway that this canker sore wouldn't stop impeding our application process, Mr. Barnside's days playing this game became numbered. Once Viken got wind of this, he became "The Spitting Dane."

One of the Selectmen in Norwell pulled me aside one evening and said, "Jeff, my daughter thinks that Friday's is the cat's ass, but I'm not going to vote for it." This was the general sentiment. Mr. Barnside's tactics couldn't go on forever, and eventually, after lots of work on our part, the board did the right thing and allowed us to proceed.

On another front, Ledger startled me one day by asking if I knew of any potential acquisition targets in the northeast. "Ryan," he said, "Let's take over a strong regional player up there. The writing is on the wall. Friday's will have saturated the market in another two years' time."

Jesus, I thought, here we were having a bit of a rough go keeping our boat from capsizing, and he wanted to take on more weight. I had to admire his gusto.

> *Flashed all their sabers bare,*
> *Flashed as they turned in air,*
> *Sab'ring the gunners there,*
> *Charging an Army,*
> *while all the world wondered.*

Word had also trickled down from Buddy's office that a Hartford restauranteur had sent a couple of his people down to Dallas to go through the Friday's management training program knowing full well that that they would go back to work for this gentleman once they graduated. Buddy's response? We'll find a location in Hartford and show the bastard! We were, in fact, already working on one just down the street.

Claus' La Jolla location would be the last one to cross the finish line in 1984, a November opening a couple of weeks before Thanksgiving.

Our travel slowed considerably as every department scrambled to get back on budget before the year's end. I had only made the one trip to Chicago with Axel to watch SMU play Notre Dame. We thought it best to take in the city for an evening and then fly back after the game.

The following Monday at the office, the boys were looking for war stories. "Not too many," I reported. They were in disbelief that we'd spent a Friday night in Chicago with nothing to report. "Well, we did take in the bar at the Alfred Lord Pick for happy hour," I said. "There was an Eastern Airlines pilot that hooked up with us who wasn't flying out until the next evening. After happy hour, he thought we ought to join him at the Pump Room on State Street since we'd never been. You won't believe this, but I was sitting in the front seat of the cab, and I could see the driver's identification card had one of those hyphenated names like Habib-Habob-Habooba or something like that so I asked "Driver, where are you from?"

"Libya." Shit. Rambo Ronnie—President Reagan—had just sent two F-111s there to take out Colonel Ghadafi! Oh boy... this could get interesting.

"What brings you to Chicago? We are here to blow up the Sears Tower!'"

"Ryan, what'd you do?" Blaze asked.

"Told him to stop the cab so we could get out!"

"Wow, makes you wonder why he'd joke like that," Sherwin observed.

"He wasn't joking!" To this day I still wonder why we did not report this guy to the authorities.

"Did you pay him?"

"Hell no! On his way out of the cab, the Eastern Airlines pilot leaned forward and asked the driver 'By the way, is it true that Ghadafi is hard of hearing?' after that he sped off!"

"So how was The Pump Room?"

"Neat spot actually. The maître'd had to bring a couple of sport coats out from the coat room in order for us to get in. Here, let me show you the back of their drink menu."

Blaze recited to the group: "'Wine, Women, and Song... If you can't sing, and you're inhibited, thank God for wine.' Mel

Brooks in The Pump Room, 29 March 1978."

"Any dollies in there?" asked Bewly.

"Actually there were two very nice gals from Green Bay that we met."

"And?"

"No runs, no hits, no errors. Got as far as a horse and buggy ride on Michigan Avenue, that's it. Lonesome Bob was the horse's name if you are looking for more details!"

"Shit, Ryan, she probably thought you were marrying material after that move."

"Believe it or not, she paged me at O'Hare the next night," I said. "Can you imagine, Axel and I are sitting at the gate and we hear, 'Jeff Ryan, please pick up the nearest red paging phone!' This was O'Hare for Pete's sake!"

"What'd she say," Bewly asked.

"Wanted to tell me what a great time she'd had, that 'if you ever get to Green Bay again,' and all that."

Blaze giggled. "The guy at the chamber of Commerce up there asked me if I knew what Green Bay was famous for other than the Packers, of course."

"What did he say?"

"He proudly said 'We happen to wipe the world's ass." Charmin is manufactured there, shouldn't everyone know that?

"How was the game?" Blaze asked.

"Oh the game was great. You all need to take that in someday. Put that in the top 20 things to do. Fellas, when the band cranks up the fight song just as they are about to enter the stadium with the students in tow! Guarantee the hair on the back of your neck will go straight up!"

"Tidy Bowl didn't lose his keys on the flight home did he?"

"No. We but we did get to sit in the Lazy Boys and watch a Robin Williams stand up performance. There was one funny sequence; Claus, you'd like this. He's playing the part of Kurt

Waldheim, the embattled Austrian Premier. About his suspected ties to The Third Reich, Robin Williams as Waldheim says, "Hey, all I know is that I had a few beers with those boys and the next thing I know, we are in Czechoslovakia! Goddamn, it was funny."

An incredible feeling came over us with the realization that we were grounded until the first of the year. Quite a shock to the system. Bewly was out every night, often taking Claus with him chasing what he referred to as "holiday hens," women he thought came out in numbers during the holidays, either making up for lost time or just searching for that elusive New Year's Eve date. For the most part, his assessment was correct. From Thanksgiving weekend on, it was nonstop. Bewly could never keep track of who was who. Betty would report to Bewly several messages a day.

Norwell was the first at bat in 1985 coming in on February 5th, again part of an aggressive schedule of somewhere between 15 and 20 store openings planned for the year depending on which way the chips fell. After Norwell, we'd have a bit of a break as the next one wasn't until Bloomington, Minnesota in May.

One day at Midway, Blaze and I were talking. "Ryan, that store is gonna be like the second coming of you know who. You won't be able to get into the joint."

Betty popped in. "Dick Leahy is on the phone."

"Thanks Betty."

Picking up the line in my office. "Hello, Dick. No, we won't be there for the opening, perhaps the week after. Let me know how our friend at The Barnside does this week. Thanks, Dick, for everything. You can buy us a scotch.... Yes, you're right, Blaze is still drinking Chivas, unless there has been a New Years resolution that I'm not aware of!"

I looked at Blaze. "Blaze, anything to report?"

He shook his head. "Dick, we're all set. Thanks again."

Sometimes I'd find myself calling the restaurant from home. If you detected a great deal of commotion in the background, you knew they were busy. "Mr. Ryan," the hostess might say, "we have been slammed since the doors opened."

Come Friday, Buddy and Viken were out in the hallway and started snickering when they noticed I was about to run The Gauntlet.

"Not bad, Ryan," Viken said. "On pace for a new opening week record." Fabulous news.

"If you get back up there," Buddy said, "give us a report."

"Roger that."

The first two weeks of business in Norwell didn't tell us much other than that some of the new employees in the back of the house were still pretty much in shock and sales were certainly not going to remain in the stratosphere. Leahy was weighing in like the true soldier that he was. "Ryan, there is a concern that the restaurant is not operating on all cylinders."

"Give it time, Dick, it has only been two weeks, I'll be out there next week to see it myself."

When we walked in together that next week, you could tell that there was panic on everyone's faces from the people on the front door to those behind the service bar. It was almost to the point where we considered chipping in and bussing tables but the food simply wasn't coming out of the kitchen.

Servers were holding up their end, putting their best foot forward and keeping patrons comfortable. The responsibility of answering questions and enduring complaints fell squarely on their shoulders.

"That's what you said ten minutes ago," said the rebellious moms sitting with fidgety children who had completely covered their place mats with drawings and were now asking to leave. It was unbearable to watch.

Sales went into a tailspin on week three. On my way back

into the office, there was no banter in the hallway. It was time to visit with Viken. "Mr. Ryan, come on in, sit down."

"Skipper," I said, "we've got to stop what we're doing." He had to hear it; it was the truth.

Taking it in, he sat back in his chair, too proud to ask tough questions, but probably wondering what we had failed to do to fill the ranks with better people. Here was a restaurant that had plenty of time to hire and train, and yet they didn't have the right crew on board. Did they know the back of the house was weak? Didn't matter; it was too late.

> *Stormed at with shot and shell,*
> *While horse and hero fell,*
> *They that had fought so well*
> *Came thro' the jaws of Death,*
> *Back from the mouth of Hell.*
> *All that was left of them,*
> *Left of six hundred.*

"Brigid," Viken called. "Schedule a trip up to Boston?" It was time for the General to leave the Chateau and visit the frontlines. Triple Six was traveling over the ground in excess of 600 MPH that morning, riding a strong tailwind. The less time inside this aluminum tube, the better. Just pass back the coffee and get through this trip!

Viken was fuming. "Buddy, listen. You guys better fix this or find somebody that can because I have no fucking clue what to do. Who is in the store right now? What the hell do we pay these Regionals for? Who's up there? Matt Kelly? What does he have to say for himself?"

"We have a bad apple in the kitchen," Buddy said.

"So here it is," Viken raged. "The kitchen? So Kelly doesn't know his ass from his elbow, is that what you are saying?" Nobody said anything. "Have we replaced anybody in the kitchen?" Viken asked. Still silence. "Can *anyone* on this airplane tell me what the hell is going on?"

Poor Matt Kelly, the lowest guy on the food chain, was going to take some severe body blows. To make matters worse, there was a bunch of snow on the ground making it difficult for Jack Wing to navigate his way to our F.B.O. He thought it best to wait for a van to drive out and guide us. This added time did not diffuse the situation one bit.

Leahy was there at lunch. "Ryan, is that the big guy?"

"Indeed."

"There isn't much he can do, is there?"

"Not really. Not unless he dawns an apron, and that isn't about to happen. There won't be a motivational speech from the top steps; I can tell you that much."

"What's your schedule Ryan?" Leahy asked.

"This is just a bullet trip with a stop in Hartford tomorrow. Trying to arrange a helicopter tour from Bradley, but I've had no luck so far."

"Where is the site in Hartford?"

"Over by Corbin's Corner. A Norwich Company wants to squeeze us in over there on the side of a cliff."

Viken took over the corner table after lunch and barked directives. "Call the guy in Hartford. Do something!"

I took shelter in the phone booth.

"Hi, David, how are we making out for tomorrow?" He was ready for us. "You are the best, David. Bell Jet Ranger at Bradley! 9a.m. Got it. See you then."

It was off to the Marriott in Copley Square where the group would reassemble for dinner at nearby Turner Fisheries. Matt Kelly, who survived the first wave, was to come in and join us.

The group assembled at a round table in the center of the restaurant, the only one that could accommodate seven people.

It felt like a theater in the round, where everyone in the room could watch the Friday's version of The Last Supper.

The affair began with martinis and small talk. No sooner had the chowders come when Viken struck a blow of desperation. "Matt, why don't you tell everyone at the table exactly what it is that you do for a living?" Viken did not stop there. "Because I really don't know myself." It was torture watching this unfold. Matt handled the pressure better than expected. Just keep your head down just like everybody else. This too shall pass!

Buddy paid the bill and then we were off to the coat check. Viken was first in line and placed his claim check along with two one dollar bills in front of the female attendant. The problem was that she was not alone; her boyfriend happened to be standing next to the door as well. Buddy, eyes rolling, saw what was coming. She wasn't exactly hustling to retrieve Viken's full length Schneider Cashmere overcoat. He was certain Viken wouldn't let this go. Sure enough, the two dollars was withdrawn from the counter and replaced with two quarters. That got her attention. "What do you think you're doing?" she accused Viken. "Well," he said, "I guess if you really give a damn whether or not I get my coat in a timely fashion, it is worth two dollars. But seeing that you don't, I believe your tip is worth a great deal less!"

He slipped on his coat and hippity hopped up the escalator en route to the Marriott bar. Over his shoulder, he yelled, "Hey, are you guys coming or aren't ya?" Our group once again took center stage at a large table. Matt, God bless him, hung with us.

When the waitress arrived, he ordered for us. "Seven Royal Salute Mists please." Perplexed, she asked Viken what the ingredients were. "Twenty-one year old Chivas over shaved ice," Viken said politely. On several occasions he was known to ask for scotch on the rocks with three ice cubes only to see if the bartender was paying attention. Needless to say, there weren't many times that his scotch arrived as ordered.

Ledge whispered to me, "Ryan, we've got to get him on the elevator."

Just then, the floor manager asked abruptly that we move the chair Matt was sitting in as it was partially blocking the aisle. This was just another opportunity for Viken to vent over what was happening thirteen miles south of the table. "Excuse me, we forgot that we were guests of your hotel."

The arrival of the Royal Salutes saved the day, and the intimidated manager moved on to greener pastures. Sans any toasts, the evening concluded for Viken, and we all watched intently as he made his way into the elevator.

Clearly Viken was just devastated at this point in time. What should have been an enjoyable, exciting moment for Fridays's, a time when the company could sit back and reap the rewards of the hard work of the past decade, was instead becoming just the opposite. Atop a pinnacle of rapid growth, Viken and the rest of us all sensed the impending precipitous decline; the crash and burn. In reality, the Norwell debacle was not just a bad hit to the company; it was worse, it was decisively the knockout punch. No longer were we the invincible army swathing a path across the country. We hadn't been totally defeated at The Battle of Norwell, but we didn't win either. Little did we know that in a year's time the entire army would be in retreat.

The phone rang early in my room the next morning. It was Ledge. "Ryan, you're not going to believe this. Viken is prancing around this morning as if nothing happened. His mood swings are something to behold, aren't they? He'd make a cup of coffee nervous. Anyway, is there any way you can get hold of your developer friend in Hartford?"

"Don't tell me the chopper ride is canceled," I said.

"No, but we would like another one. Seems everyone is coming back with us."

"Ledge, do you realize what it took for me to get one whirlybird?"

"Alright, well, hey, give it your best shot and call me back."

With just an hours notice, I called up David Mills, a terrific guy and very much liked by Fridays's.

"Don't tell me you're not coming—" he began.

"No, we are coming alright, but the passenger list has gotten larger."

In a bewildered voice, "Not another helicopter."

"I know this is asking a lot, but I was hoping just this one time." Incredibly, he returned to the phone with good news.

"Ryan, okay, there happens to be another one that just dropped someone off. Hey, make sure when we board that Viken goes with me."

"Roger that, see you in an hour or so."

On the way to Logan, Viken was chirping like a sick duck's ass. "Ryan, how many Aerospatiales do we have at our disposal this morning?"

"You mean Bell Jet Rangers? Just two."

"Are we going to fly over this guy's restaurant? The one who sent his manager down to us?"

"Oh yeah. He's over there at Corbin's Corner. Right down the street from us."

Bradley was pretty much deserted when we arrived that chilly morning. There were the two choppers side by side with David, our savior, who greeted everyone. However, before he was able to assume the role of tour guide, the incorrigible Viken scampers out on the tarmac and climbs into one of the waiting whirlybirds. Chagrinned, David turned to me to say, "Ryan, all the maps are in the other chopper. Can you ask him if he wouldn't mind going in the other one?" Knowing the answer was a foregone conclusion, I asked none the less. The now playful Viken slid back the tiny window. "Hey Skip, David wants you to go with him in the other bird. There are points of interest he would like to show you."

"That's okay," Viken said. "He and I will talk later."

"David, this is hard to explain, however, he is in a genuinely ball-busting mood this morning. He must have gotten a good night's sleep. Stay with us!"

"Ryan," David said, moving on, "okay, we don't have permission, however we are going to try to set down on the peripheral property of West Farms Mall. We should have enough time to walk across the street before Taubman's people tell us we are not welcome." Sounded like he had it all figured out; I trusted him. Off we went in tight formation. We did not realize it then, but this was the last of the Whirlybird rides. Perhaps Viken had some sense of this and his attitude was a product of that; on the other hand, perhaps I'm giving him too much credit. In any event, this was it.

Mall security didn't get wind of our arrival until we had walked across the street. Can you imagine what was radioed in from that parking lot? "Parking lot to base, Two Bell Jet Rangers just landed on our peripheral property. Seven unknowns are walking across New Britain Avenue. Enroute to speak with the pilots. Standby."

Viken didn't give a shit about looking at a piece of dirt. Instead, he wanted to walk down to BT 11's, the restaurant that was under construction. The Magnificent Seven marched single file the short distance down the street. It seemed the circus had arrived. The construction workers must have thought that we were inspectors. The owner came and introduced himself.

"Can I help you gentlemen?"

This time Viken took center stage. "Not really, we're from T.G.I.Friday's. We just wanted to see who our competition was."

"You mean Dallas Friday's?" he asked.

"Yes," Viken said. "We're going to open up right down the street."

There was a lump forming in this guy's throat.

"You're building two floors here I see?" observed Viken.

"Yes," the owner said. "Going to be big."

"Where's the elevator?" Viken asked. The owner looked around but didn't answer. "Well, good luck!" Viken said, and with that we left.

"Oh boy," Ledge said, "this guy's shitting a brick."

"That elevator snafu is going to cost that asshole bigtime! Look at the security forces surrounding the helicopters. We best hightail it out of here before the police arrive," Viken said.

At Bradley, we thanked David for his efforts. "Viken, we are planning on refueling at Fairfield," said Buddy.

"Something about strong headwinds going back."

"Have Jack call ahead and order a couple of pizzas from Chester's and ice down a couple of cases of PBR's." Roger that! Triple Six put down at Fairfield County Airport outside of Cincinnati. Viken had Jack place one of the pizzas in the nose storage compartment. Jack proudly observed, "It'll be frozen by the time we reach the hangar, just like you want it." Always thinking of the details.

The following Monday, Blaze was already there when I came into the office. "Good morning. How was your trip?"

"A little bit out of the ordinary you might say." It had felt different, for sure. None of us knew what was in store for the company at that point. But the trip up to Boston had given us all the sense that things would somehow change.

"Wish I could have been there with you guys." I noticed a letter on the center of my desk. No envelope; just a letter on Friday's linen stationery. It was from Viken, dated March 5, 1986 It read: "Dear Jeffrey, Congratulations on reaching your five year anniversary with our company. It is because of your effort and the efforts of others like you that Friday's is so tremendously successful. In appreciation, please accept this ring as an expression of my gratitude for your contributions over the past five years." Viken had signed it. I've always kept this as a reminder of what we achieved and what Friday's meant to each of us.

Staring at the ceiling with my feet propped up on my desk, letter in my left hand down to my side, my emotions were just about to get the better of me. Just then, one by one, Bewly, Claus, Betty, and Sherwin marched in to offer congratulations.

Suddenly the phones started to ring. It would be 9:00 on the east coast. Blaze answered. "Good morning, Mr. Fabbiano. I see; a site in Stamford?" I started snapping my fingers to get his attention. "Uh, let me transfer you, to the person who conducts helicopter tours of Connecticut for us. His name is Mr. Ryan." I picked up. "Hey, Larry, you remember Blaze. Sure, we can meet on Wednesday. Dinner in the city? Now you're talking. See you then, Larry."

Buddy examined the 85 schedule and then glanced up at our map of the Northeast. "Ryan," he said, "great job up there. Couldn't have done it out without you."

"You taught me well."

"Always the optimistic one! Go up to New York and let it fly!" Blaze said, cigarette dangling from the corner of his mouth.

Larry took to me to Sparks Steakhouse for a late lunch to celebrate the Huntington deal. As we approached the maitre'd, Larry wisecracked, "Two for the No Shooting Section."

"Right this way, sir." Sparks didn't need the extra attention of a Gambino family mob hit outside their front door. It was already a world renowned steakhouse. Sitting down, I recalled something. "Larry, we should have asked Linus to join us."

"I did, but he said that he couldn't handle another night out with you!"

"Well, a toast to him in absentia," I said. After the conclusion of our luncheon meeting, I headed back on the L.I.E. to LaGuardia, only to discover traffic was backed up for miles. There was no chance for me to make the 6 o'clock, but there was an outside shot at making the 8 o'clock out of J.F.K.

"Ryan, go up to New York and let it fly," Blaze's words replayed in my head. A sign above the most attractive KLM gate agent displayed: Amsterdam—7:30 departure. "Good evening. How about one ringside?"

She winked. "Let me see what I can come up with. Aha!" With a few swift moves, once again the welcome sound of the boarding pass spitting out from below. "Mr. Ryan, do you have a place to stay when you arrive?"

"Glad you asked. What do you suggest?"

She smiled. "The Amstel Hotel. In fact, I can see to your reservation if you like."

"That would be fantastic," I said. Finding a pay phone, "Hello, Betty, it's me, Ryan. Do me a favor, if you don't mind."

"Sure, what is it?" she asked.

"Cover for me. I'll be back on Tuesday. I'll tell you all about it then.

On the flight over, I got to thinking about what would happen to everyone.

A flight attendant came by and asked "Good Evening, Mr. Ryan. Can I get you anything to drink?" My hotel reservation paper was on my lap, Amstel Hotel in capital letters. "How about a Heineken?"

"Certainly," she said, handing me a bottle.

 Back at Midway on Monday, they'd be a man short, and though I'd be back Tuesday, we'd all soon move on to other things. Without a doubt, we had succeeded on our mission and achieved unprecedented success in our ranks. We had experienced quite the ride along the way.

When can their glory fade,
Oh, the wild charge they made!

As the flight attendant continued down the aisle, I caught myself looking into her cart to see if there was any Chivas in it. But things were changing, and I was traveling alone now.